Debbie McDonald

Riding Through

An Olympic medalist's
lessons on life and dressage

PRIMEDIA
EQUINE
NETWORK

First Published in 2006 by PRIMEDIA Equine Network
656 Quince Orchard Road, #600
Gaithersburg, MD 20878
301-977-3900

VP, Group Publishing Director: Susan Harding
Editorial Director: Cathy Laws
Director, Product Marketing: Julie Beaulieu

Printed in the USA.

Book Design: Lauryl Suire Eddlemon
Production: Lara Pinson

Photography
Front cover photo: PhelpsPhotos®.com
Back cover photo: Elma Garcia
Photo page 6: courtesy Jen Serot
Photo page 7: Lawrence J. Nagy
Photos pages 9, 10, 11, 12, 71: courtesy Debbie McDonald
Photo page 67: PhelpsPhotos®.com
Photo page 74: Susan J. Stickle
Photo page 95: CLIX
Photo page 100: Jan Gyllensten
All other photos: Nancy Jaffer

Order by calling 800-952-5813 or online at www.HorseBooksEtc.com

Library of Congress Cataloging-in-Publication Data

McDonald, Debbie.
  Riding through : an Olympic medalist's guide to dressage / by Debbie
McDonald, with Nancy Jaffer.
     p. cm.
  ISBN-13: 978-1-929164-35-6
  1. Dressage. I. Jaffer, Nancy. II. Title.
  SF309.5.M43 2006
  798.2'3—dc22

                              2006028292

Debbie McDonald and her book's reader/riders: Left to right, Wendy Wisz, Kathi Young, Linda Fowler, Paola Diem, Elaine Lindo, Kim Opiatowski.

Acknowledgments

The authors are very grateful for the help of Jane Thomas, Adrienne Lyle and Tracy Roenick, who graciously posed for many of the photos that illustrate this book. In addition, we want to thank a spirited group of reader/riders who offered opinions and suggestions along the way—Kim Opiatowski, Elaine Lindo, Wendy Wisz, Paola Diem, Kathi Young and Linda Fowler. Bob McDonald also gave freely of his considerable expertise, which helped this project along, and Larry Nagy was, as always, a most patient listener. We very much appreciate the assistance of Beth Baumert, technical editor of *Dressage Today*, who contributed excellent suggestions.

We remain in the debt of Peggy and Parry Thomas for their continued support, hospitality, guidance and vision, which are at the root of everything that this book is about.

There are too many other people to list who have contributed a great deal along the way to a very special horse and her rider. Love and thanks to them; they know who they are.

Contents

Introduction

THERE IS MORE THAN ONE REASON THAT I CALL THIS BOOK "RIDING THROUGH." Of course, first and foremost, riding through is a dressage term, something you strive for as you attempt to get your horse on the aids and moving back-to-front. You have achieved it when everything the two of you do together is one fluid motion, the ultimate of coordination and expression, in which the horse is maximizing his assets. It's all about harmony and correctness, summing up the meaning of dressage in a single short phrase.

But "riding through" has other meanings for me as well. I've learned to ride through hard times, on and off a horse, when I thought about giving up. We all have to learn about riding through, because that's the only way we will arrive at our destination, whatever it may be.

In the biography chapters of this book, you'll learn about my personal experiences, and the way riding through, in every sense, brought me to where I am today.

In the how-to chapters, I'll help you train your horse and yourself the way I train, using simple building blocks, common sense, respect for the horse and hard work to achieve a goal. What that goal is doesn't matter—this isn't a book only for those who aspire to doing a perfect piaffe, though I'm happy to assist you toward that end, too.

If you haven't done much riding, however, read the biography sections, then put this book aside, take some basic lessons, and come back to it. I'm not starting you from scratch, so you'll need a little bit of background in the saddle to make use of what I have to say.

Once you get that, we'll have fun working together, no matter what your orientation. Trail riders can make their horses more responsive with the simple ring work and exercises for achieving sensitivity to the aids. A leg-yield or shoulder-in is a great distraction if your horse is acting up along a path in the woods.

Even those who prefer a western saddle will be able to take some of the principles I set out and do better in their pursuits, as communication between horse and rider improves. Hunter and jumper riders, you'll find your horses are more adjustable if they have some dressage basics. Equitation riders, you'll be able to ride shoulder-in and a neat turn on the haunches for those work-offs. Eventers, you know that with the evolution of cross-country, dressage has become far more important at the upper levels of your sport, the way it has been for some years at the lower levels, too. The comment, "she finished on her dressage score" is often seen in the write-ups of winners from novice level to advanced.

I embarked on a whole new life— and understanding of horses—when I got serious about dressage.

And for those of you who are interested in really pursuing dressage as an end, I hope you'll find a lot that can help you in this book. Dressage is a wonderful discipline with so much to explore. Starting as practically a rank beginner in what seemed to me at the time an exotic pastime, with just my experience in the hunter/jumper ranks to draw on, I embarked on a whole new life—and understanding of horses—when I got serious about dressage.

Along the way, I have been to so many interesting places around the world and had such marvelous experiences, more than I ever dreamed of in my childhood fantasies during the years that I was riding my pony bareback in Orange County, California.

And I've been introduced to so many such wonderful people, too. Of course, they include all of today's dressage riders and master teachers, but there have been others you have never heard of who have meant as much, or even more, to me. One with whom I have a special relationship is Jennifer Serot, the cancer-stricken teen who told the Make-A-Wish Foundation that she wanted to meet me. That wish came true, as did another—she got better and today is a lovely young lady whose cancer is in remission. We e-mail each other nearly every day, and I am so thankful to my sport for bringing her into my life.

Brentina and I with Jen Serot, a close friend who we met through the Make-A-Wish Foundation.

I also am extremely grateful to my sponsors, Peggy and Parry Thomas, for enabling me to do everything that I've done, and to their daughter, Jane, for her continued support. Needless to say, without the help of my family—my husband, Bob, who has been with me all the way on this exciting venture into dressage; our son, Ryan; and step-daughter, Kim Koch; I probably would have given up long ago.

Of course, dressage has also made it possible for me to establish such wonderful relationships with my horses, especially the valiant Beaurivage, who gave me my start at the Grand Prix level, and Brentina, who is as close to me as a horse can be to a human. She's my other half in the show ring, and I can't imagine that I would have made it to the Olympics or World Championships without her.

As you and I get ready to begin our time together, I want to emphasize that you must be clear and focused when you work with your horse. Everything is black and white to horses, and I've found most problems in the ring are rider-induced, a lack of communication between horse and rider.

You will need to lay down some serious ground rules in your training, and stick with them. You can't say, "I'm only going to be a Training Level rider, so I can let my horse get away with stuff." If you do, you'll find that before long, you won't even be able to ride Training Level.

Our work requires serious commitment. I made mine by writing this book. I hope you will find my instruction and advice helpful, and that it advances your cause in the saddle. Maybe someday, we can talk some more at one of the clinics I give around the country. Until then, try to follow the guidelines I've laid out, considering it a conversation with you, me and your horse.

Foreword

DEBBIE MCDONALD HAS NEVER SEEN ME RIDE, BUT SHE'S THE BEST TRAINER I ever had. Though she will never see most of you ride either, my expectation is that after you finish this book, you and your horse will have benefited from a learning experience similar to mine.

When I started this project, I didn't really expect to pick up much that I could apply to my own riding. After all, my showing days (when I did a lot of jumping and a little dressage; most particularly, eventing dressage) are long past because of work demands. But by talking with Debbie and understanding her methods, I have learned so much that has made my "difficult" horse less so, and taught me to become a thinking rider who feels safer in the saddle on our adventurous trail rides.

At the beginning of my association with Debbie, I was always asking her, "How should I react if my horse does this?" or "What's the best strategy if my horse does that?"

I'll never forget the day recently when I was having trouble with my horse repeatedly spooking at one spot in the ring, and I figured out how to handle it on my own, based on Debbie's system. It was an exciting breakthrough moment for me, leading to a whole new way of reacting to problems when I ride.

So this book isn't just for the accomplished dressage rider, or someone who aspires to that designation. While we feel it will be very useful for those readers, there are many others who can benefit from the lessons it teaches. A group of reader/riders at several different levels has reviewed what we've written to make sure we're answering a wide range of needs with this volume.

We're particularly targeting the rider who already has some experience and may even have started dressage—or is contemplating doing it. Other potential readers include eventers who want to improve their dressage scores, or equitation riders who need better flatwork to make a strong impression in the USEF Talent Search and other classes. Perhaps you just want your horse to go better in a discipline you already are pursuing, such as the hunters, jumpers or even the pleasure division. Maybe, like me, all you want is for your horse to respond better to you and give you a safer, smoother experience on the trails. This book can help.

Grand Prix aspirants should get some ideas and inspiration, too, though they will have to rely on the assistance of a trainer who can watch them and their horses on a regular basis in order to achieve their goals.

Nancy Jaffer and Spectacular Gift

Do you need an issue solved? There's a good chance you'll find the answers in these pages. After all, Debbie's motto is: "Don't worry, we can fix it."

This book does not take as clinical an approach as many "how to" offerings do these days, with a step-by-step format throughout. We decided to present Debbie's instruction in a more conversational tone, so it fits in better with the biography chapters, which are scattered through the book. I know you will be as fascinated and inspired by Debbie's story as I am, and that you will get to know her so well in *Riding Through* that you will feel she's with you when you're riding.

People often ask me if Debbie is as nice as her image. The answer is an unqualified "Yes." She is fun, generous, kind and above all, a woman who really loves horses, rather than simply using them as a means to a goal—something I've seen too often in horse sport these days. Her relationship with Brentina tells you everything you need to know about Debbie. The two of them could not be as close as they are if Debbie were not as good-hearted and genuine as she is.

I've also received a fringe benefit from this project in getting to know the people close to Debbie, including her husband, Bob, who has played such a big role in her success; her sponsors, the very hospitable Peggy and Parry Thomas and their gracious daughter, Jane; Debbie's talented working student, Adrienne Lyle, and her wonderful barn staff, especially the dedicated Ruben Palomera; Antonio Pina, who shares my love of cats, and the hard-working Juan Ruiz.

I hope you find what you seek in this book, and enjoy your time with Debbie as much as I have!

Nancy Jaffer

P.S. I should mention that even though Brentina is a mare, for the sake of simplicity, we refer to other horses as "he" throughout the book.

CHAPTER 1

How I Got Started

ON A LOVELY SPRING MORNING AT THE 1988 Del Mar, California, Horse Show, I was warming up a pre-green hunter, one of the nicest horses my husband, Bob, and I had ever come across.

Nothing was out of the ordinary; it was just another day at the office for me, a professional hunter/jumper rider married to a trainer who bought and sold horses for a living. But in one moment, everything changed completely. I would end up saying goodbye to the pleasant, if unremarkable, life I had carved out, exchanging it for an extraordinary destiny that would send me to incredible places I had never dreamed of going.

It all started with nothing more than a "swoosh" as a water truck went by the warm-up arena, only minutes before I was to enter the nearby ring for my competition. The mare was just beginning to leave the ground at the base of an unassuming 2-foot, 6-inch vertical obstacle when the noise of the truck startled her.

Here I am on Fridolin, a successful working hunter.

She tried to put her feet back down before jumping, but instead wound up straddling a rail she had just dislodged, tripping her.

The jolt sent me flying out of the saddle, thrown way in front of her when I hit the ground. I landed hard, face first, but for an instant, seemingly out of harm's way. Then, while I rolled over to get up, I saw the mare's nose dip into the dirt and she flipped completely over, as if in horrific slow motion. Her whole back end crashed down on me. What saved my life was that the massive 17-hand horse hit me from the neck down, rather than landing on my head. Struggling to get up, she thrashed back and forth on me a couple of times before she was able to find her feet.

Almost instantly, intense pain seeped into my consciousness and I came to the sickening realization that I was in big trouble. I remember thinking that if the mare didn't get up quickly, I was going to die. It all happened in a matter of a few frightening seconds, but it felt like an excruciating eternity before her weight finally lifted off me.

"I thought you were dead," one person who witnessed the accident told me later, but the extent of my distress wasn't as obvious to everyone else, apparently.

"Just sit there a minute before you think about getting back on," Bob told me matter-of-factly after he ran over to see how I was. Barely able to speak, I told him through sharp, jagged breaths, "There's no way I'm getting back on; I think I'm really hurt."

Somehow, though, I struggled to my feet and agonizingly edged into the golf cart that we used for getting around the extensive show grounds. I should have just stayed quiet until an ambulance came. But falls are so common at shows that we all were used to soldiering on when we ached after a spill.

Amazingly, I managed to get from the golf cart into one of our customer's cars. Bob had to stay at the show to help the other riders from our barn, so the customer took me to the hospital, where emergency-room doctors gave me medication. They also monitored me to make sure there was no serious internal bleeding—which was hard to believe, considering the extent of my injuries.

The doctors told me I had a broken rib, a ruptured spleen, an injured shoulder and bruising of some internal organs. It wasn't until much later that they discovered I also had chipped a vertebra in my neck. It, in turn, would herniate a disc, which led to neck surgery a few months later, and I needed shoulder surgery several times as well.

But that wasn't apparent then, so only hours after the accident, I went back to the horse show, watching the horses I was supposed to compete on being ridden by someone else. Though everything seemed normal, it wasn't. More than my injuries were troubling me on that day and the ones to follow, a misery combining physical pain and fear.

Five years before, I had become a mother, and our son, Ryan, was the center of my life. His birth completely changed my perspective. I'm sure every mother feels this way; you realize you're there for somebody other than yourself.

Three weeks after the accident, I started riding again, but it wasn't the same. That instinctive feel and comfort level for the right moment to take off over a jump had vanished. Every time a horse left the ground with me, I felt very apprehensive. I realized I was losing my nerve.

"I can't do this anymore," I told my husband more than once. Eventually, he agreed with me, admitting I was getting too "safe," failing to let the horse jump at the optimum moment if we were just a little long to the best departure point.

It seemed inevitable that given the circumstances and my ever-increasing lack of nerve, I was going to have another serious accident if I kept on jumping.

The thought of a life without riding made me feel even worse. I had loved horses since my early childhood, when we traveled from my Orange County, California, home to visit relatives in Kansas every summer. The long car trip was hard for a little girl, but the pot of gold at the end of that rainbow was the fact that there was always a horse or pony waiting for me. It was then that I realized I had a huge spot in my heart for horses. I just couldn't stop thinking about them.

Every time a horse left the ground with me, I felt very apprehensive. I realized I was losing my nerve.

This is Ryan as a baby.

At home, a friend and I would go to the Back Bay area near Santa Ana to ride horses at a local stable. Of course, we had no instruction, but we loved our time on the trails. What we didn't love, however, was watching other riders take off their belts and beat the tired, well-worn hack horses to make them gallop. It sickened us, because we loved those horses so.

After the trail ride, we'd hang out at the stable and brush the rental mounts. I don't think they ever had that luxury before, and they enjoyed our gentle grooming. But occasional outings to this stable weren't enough for me. I wanted my own horse, and so did my girlfriend. It seemed like the impossible dream, as many childhood fantasies are, but it was even more unreachable for me.

My father had suffered a pretty severe heart attack and was disabled, so my stay-at-home mom became a secretary in her 40s, earning barely enough to keep us going. That made it very difficult for me to ask my parents for money for a pony, but I did it anyway. Of course, I knew times were tough, but since 12-year-olds don't have any real concept of money, I showed my dad a newspaper ad for a $400 pony.

"I would love for you to have this pony, but we can't afford it," he told me sadly. He explained that buying the pony wasn't so much the problem; it was the cost of keeping it.

I thought a moment and then asked my father, "What if I can find a way to pay for the board?"

"At your age?" he asked with a skeptical smile, thinking he had put the matter to rest.

I wasn't going to be dissuaded, however. My pal did wind up buying a $500 horse she found in the classified ads, and I made friends with the people who had the small backyard barn where she kept her purchase.

I confided to the barn owners that I was looking for a pony, and wondered if there was any way I could work off my board. When they said yes, my father agreed to pay the purchase price, but said the rest was up to me. Though the original pony was gone by that time, there was an ad for another $400 pony in the paper with the romantic name of Flannigan's Falling Star. We gelded the little Welsh stallion, and I earned his keep by doing chores, mucking stalls and cleaning up after dogs at the backyard stable.

My friend and I had a blast, riding her horse and my pony like little Indians in the Back Bay. Then we ran into someone who was into showing, and went to watch her compete in a gymkhana at the Orange County Fairgrounds.

We were fascinated and got into showing too, riding our horses an hour to the fairgrounds, competing all day, and then riding an hour home.

I quickly decided it would be more fun to be stabled at the show grounds, a vast facility where there was every type of horse and riding, from Hackneys and Appaloosas to jumping and western.

The only place I could find a stall, however, was at a saddle-horse trainer's barn. It cost $250 a month, and I knew

Flannigan's Falling Star played a big role in my young life.

I couldn't go to my parents for that money. So I walked around the fairgrounds asking if I could clean stalls, and soon was making an average of $350 a month, cleaning 10 to 20 stalls a day.

I didn't mind the mucking, but getting the manure into the dumpsters was a problem. I was tiny, just 5 feet tall, and pushing the heavy wheelbarrows up the ramp took all the strength I had. By the end of the day, when I was tired, my muscles failed me and sometimes the wheelbarrow would go off the side of the ramp, tipping its contents all over. So I'd have to clean up the manure and start again.

Meanwhile, I wasn't happy with my pony's accommodations, because the trainer was a strange guy who kept all his horses in the dark. He'd go in the stalls and start screaming and yelling at his animals, who would stand in the back blowing and snorting like fire-eating dragons. He loved that, but his tactics made me cringe, and I warned him never to touch my pony.

One day, however, I showed up unexpectedly to find him in my pony's stall, brandishing a whip. Talk about hysterical! I grabbed the pony's halter, took him out of there and started scouring the show grounds, tearfully asking anybody I saw if they had stalls available. A young man named Bob McDonald took one look at my tear-stained face and found a stall for my pony. That's how Bob and I actually met. He was married at the time and had a 4-year-old daughter; I was 14.

Bob McDonald took one look at my tear-stained face and found a stall for my pony. That's how Bob and I actually met.

Bob in the show ring.

I started working for him in my specialty, cleaning stalls. When I got extra money, I took jumping lessons on his school horses. After riding a little pony for several years, I had no idea how to stay on a horse and spent much of my lesson hours falling off. It was a running joke at the Orange County Fairgrounds: "Let's go see Debbie take her jumping lesson and bet how many times she'll go off today."

By this time, it was obvious I had outgrown my pony, Flannigan's Falling Star. Bob advised me to get a horse, but I couldn't afford it. So he helped me sell the pony for $1,000. Since my first horse cost only $800, I gave my parents the $200 profit from the sale to partially repay them for their initial investment in the pony.

Though selling my pony was a sad moment, it also marked the start of what would soon become a business for me. Because I didn't have the money for horse-show entry fees, another girl who could afford it competed my horses while I groomed for her. Showing made my horses more valuable, which meant I could sell them and use the money to buy something new to groom, train and sell.

Bob, who has a great eye for potential equine talent, would find me prospects that looked as if they were on their last legs—skinny and unattractive, with long, unkempt coats and tangled manes. More than anything, I loved turning those horses into swans. I would groom them forever and do everything I could to make them look good, filling them with nutritious feed, alfalfa and molasses. Even today, some of the most fun moments I have involve spending that kind of time with my horses–bathing, clipping and just hanging out with them.

Though buying and selling got to be a very successful business for me, I wanted to keep one horse forever. I was tired of getting attached to them and selling them. Then we found this great Thoroughbred, Ask Anyone. He was my keeper, as well as my ticket to getting established as a rider. I showed this talented horse very successfully in the Regular Working Hunter and 4-foot Conformation Hunter divisions.

That was about the time that Peggy and Parry Thomas started to sponsor my riding. The Thomases were long-time customers of Bob's, who had taught the couple's daughter, Jane, since she was 9 years old. When Jane was getting ready to go to college and take a break from horses, I moved from the amateur division into the open classes and began showing her family's investment horses.

I hadn't gone to college; in fact, I barely got through high school. I just didn't fit in at the school in exclusive Newport Beach, where I attended classes because we happened to live nearby in a far less fancy neighborhood. I couldn't wait for the day high school was finally over so I could be with the horses full time.

Jane Thomas and her parents, Peggy and Parry, with me in one of our outdoor rings.

A lot changed after I graduated. I became Bob's assistant trainer. He and his wife got divorced. Although she originally was interested in horses, she was going in a different direction and they separated amicably, originally sharing custody of their 9-year-old daughter, Kim.

A few years after Bob got divorced, he and I were both at the barn late, and he asked me if I wanted to go to a horse sale with him. Of course I said yes; I had been in love with him since I was 14 and he gave my pony a home. In fact, for some strange reason at that time, I knew I was going to be with Bob for the rest of my life. After the auction, we went out to dinner, so I guess you could consider that our first date.

Soon we were married, and Kim came to live with us because she was interested in horses. I consider her my daughter. And I'm friends with Bob's ex-wife, Sue, so it's all worked out quite well.

Bob and I had a very comfortable existence until my accident, buying and selling the horses I showed. Our business focused on dealing in young horses, however, and they needed a rider who was sure of herself to guide them as they began showing. A year after my fall, I finally gave up jumping. I wasn't ready to give up riding, though, and that's when we made the very difficult decision that I should switch to dressage.

Bob and I at Redfish Lake near our home.

Brentina and I have a very special relationship.

That way, I could still compete and be part of our business, but at no risk. Though we knew almost nothing about dressage, Bob thought with his usual perceptiveness that it looked like an interesting sport, one that was going places.

Peggy Thomas was involved in dressage, which turned out to be very helpful. While I was apprehensive, she was delighted to hear I would be joining her in the discipline. But when I first sat in a dressage saddle, massive compared to my little jumping saddle, my first thought was, "There's no way. There's so much leather here I can't get a feel of the horse."

And after I was told I had to learn to sit the trot, my next thought was "Oh, my God!"

The Thomases had a horse, Willie the Great, being trained by 1984 Olympic rider Hilda Gurney. She came up to our Idaho home from California occasionally to teach Peggy, and she started me in dressage. After a few lessons, it was time to get serious.

To develop my seat, I was sent to her farm for grueling hours on the longe line. It was awful. There was, it turned out, nothing fun about trying to learn a new sport when you've been successful in a different one. I didn't think I was going to enjoy dressage. Boy, was I wrong.

I learned to love it, and you will too, as you follow the pointers I give you in the chapters to come. This book is geared for someone with a little riding experience in another discipline, so you'll find your basic knowledge and background with horses will help you along.

Together, we'll make it happen, and along the way, I'll share my story. You'll understand it wasn't easy for me at first, either, but applying yourself to this challenging and interesting discipline can bring so many rewards for you and your horse. Even if you never make it as far as Second Level, you'll still have fun, I promise!

Let's Ride

Brentina and I spend a lot of time together, continuing to forge the bond that has helped us succeed in the show ring.

CHAPTER 2

Getting You Started

IN DRESSAGE, YOU'RE TEACHING YOUR HORSE MOVEMENTS SUCH AS PASSAGE AND PIAFFE that they might do in the wild if they're excited. But without training, they certainly would not offer those movements willingly to a rider. What makes dressage training so challenging is that you need to keep your horse excited and willing to give you all these things without damaging his character and personality. It's a very fine line, and one that takes a long time to draw well.

Even if passage and piaffe aren't your ambition, or you don't want to compete in dressage at any level, the good basic riding skills involved in learning this discipline will help you in whatever you want to do with horses—whether it's improving adjustability for jumping or just having a more pleasurable trail ride. And the challenges will keep you interested while you explore the very special connection that develops between human and horse when you're doing meaningful work together.

So here we go: I'd like to share with you what I've learned about dressage over the years. I didn't have consistent help in the very beginning, which meant a lot of what I learned (and sometimes had to re-learn the right way), happened by trial and error. I want to make things smoother for you, with a system that has worked for me and can work for you, too.

Even though I had good basics as an A-rated-show hunter/jumper rider, I realized the dressage seat was something very different, and applied myself to learning it. The seat provides the base and security for everything else you do. Be aware that developing it will take time, so don't get discouraged. You have to be patient to cultivate a correct seat. Sometimes, that means lessons on the longe line without stirrups, painful hours you spend trying to get balanced and find the place where you need to sit. The goal is an independent leg, seat and hand, so when you take hold of your reins, you're not gripping frantically with your legs and cruising for an explosion. At first, it may seem as difficult as patting your head and rubbing your tummy at the same time, but it can be done.

Try this approach if you have somebody you trust, with a good eye for a correct seat, at the other end of that longe line. If that doesn't suit you, or it's not possible in your situation, mirrors are important tools to help you check what you are doing. We have included photos in this book that can show you the correct way to position yourself for maximum effect, but you should also try to watch your trainer or experienced competitors ride to get the whole picture.

Dressage represents an amazing relationship between a horse and rider. Because it's necessary to spend so many hours and years developing dressage horses, I have a stronger bond and better relationship with them than I ever had with any horse I rode during my career with hunters and jumpers. That's due to the long and intense training involved.

Look in the mirror often to check your position and see what your horse is doing.

Don't take any short cuts. The right seat is the foundation for developing your confidence, so you have the proper basis to do all the things we're going to explore together. When we're finished, you'll be a better rider, and you'll be able to give your partner, the horse, a chance to reach his maximum potential.

Not every horse can make it to Grand Prix—in dressage *or* show jumping, for that matter—but I'm confident you can improve every horse if you use these guidelines.

What follows is a section on "Perfecting the Basics," the foundation for all the work you'll be doing in dressage. It includes my explanation of the movements you need as the underpinning for what you're going to do. As you go along, you'll also find my "recipes" for those movements, arranged so you can refer to them easily when you need them, without having to hunt through long blocks of text.

I've tried to make the recipes as simple as possible, covering what the movement is, what it does and how it fits into the overall training scheme, along with some

helpful hints and words of warning. Keep going back to them. They should enable you to become familiar with what you need to know for progress in "making" a horse who is happy and willing to work for you.

Take as long as you need to get the basics. Even upper-level competitors ride these movements daily. If you're having trouble getting your horse on the bit at the trot, you're not alone. Professionals struggle with issues at the upper levels, too. There is always more to learn and there are always more ways to achieve that knowledge.

I preach daily to the people I teach, telling them as they go up the levels, "You have to go back to where the connection is correct, the horse is on the aids and you can stretch him long and low in every movement." Long and low means bringing the horse's head forward and down after collection or hard work, and still keeping your connection.

If at some point you feel you're struggling and frustrated, the first thing I would ask you is, "Do you have an eye on the ground? Are you working with a trainer?" If the answer is no, get someone to help you for a while at least.

A good trainer is your eye on the ground and will help you get the most out of your horse.

Joey, with my assistant Adrienne Lyle up, is in a nice frame for a young horse. He's relaxed and stretching forward, but doesn't have his nose out as far as he will when he's more developed; he was only four when this photo was taken.

Another barrier to success can be lack of fitness. You need to have good core strength. Sometimes, I'll take a horse's reins and say to the rider in the saddle, "Don't let me pull you forward." But more times than not, their legs go back and "whoops." That's when you start to learn where your core strength is, so you can hold your position in the saddle.

Core strength is more known in today's world than it used to be through the popularity of Pilates. I know people who had problems with their backs and shoulders who started Pilates and they cannot believe how much they've developed in their riding through core strength. I developed core strength early, probably by cleaning 20 stalls a day when I was a kid. I've always been a fireplug, short but strong in my upper body. I danced when I was younger, and that must have helped develop core strength and balance, too.

It's difficult to stay in shape just by riding three times a week. Unless you can afford multiple horses and take more than a few lessons weekly, you need to add trips to a gym. I go to Curves. It's amazing what it does to tone your body.

WHAT YOU'LL NEED

Before you get started, you will have to get a few things that are essential to help you with the training process and prepare for competition. Number one is the right saddle; it must not only be comfortable for you, but also comfortable for your horse. So many saddles don't fit properly, causing the horse a lot of pain. When horses are in pain, they're not willing to work, so you'll get resistance that is unfair to address through discipline.

Dressage saddles are expensive. But your local tack shop undoubtedly has access to used saddles, and perhaps someone can even come and fit your horse if you're unsure of how the saddle should rest on his back. It's important that you're sitting in the center of your horse with your legs properly underneath you. Not all saddles (jumping, all-purpose, western) work for the movements you will learn in this book; a dressage saddle is built for them.

The bridle is simple; you'll start with a plain snaffle. I prefer the loose-ring KK variety. Experiment a little, borrowing bits from friends to hold down costs, until you find something that keeps your horse's mouth quiet and moist. Then you can buy it.

To protect your horse's legs, you may consider boots or bandages. You should use bell boots when riding a young horse in the gawky stage, because he might have a tendency to overreach and hurt himself. If you see a horse with bell boots on all four feet, that probably indicates the horse travels close, which means he could bruise one leg with another.

For leg protection, in Europe they're fond of a thin quilt under a cotton bandage. In this country, a lot of people use polo wraps, which are thicker than the cotton bandage itself. If you have a horse that does interfere, more padding will be helpful in keeping him from bruising himself.

When a horse is well balanced and shod properly with no interfering problem, boots, rather than wraps, are totally sufficient for protecting from any unforeseen incident like a spook, when the horse might bump himself. They also take less time to put on than wraps.

Another necessity is a dressage whip, which is longer than the whip you used in show jumping or going cross-country. Feel free to pick up something very inexpensive at a discount tack store that will do the trick.

When it comes to your boots, you probably already have a pair if you showed in the hunters, jumpers and equitation, or if you evented. They'll do fine at the lower levels. When you get ready for new boots, though, remember that the hunter/jumper boots are designed to enable you to drop your heel deeply in short stirrups. In dressage, to be effective, your leg must hang longer, so it lies differently on the saddle. There should be a straight line from your shoulder to your hip and your heel, with just a little bit of weight in your heel. (Don't make the mistake of lengthening your stirrups so much that you're hanging on with your toe, though!) The stiffer leather boots used for dressage help promote the proper leg and foot position. How you hold your legs will vary, of course. You don't always have your leg "on." Keep your leg relaxed, putting it on only when you need to and using the spur as a stronger prompt if your horse doesn't respond (see photos on pages 22 and 23).

Through Fourth Level, you can wear the approved helmet with a chinstrap that you used in hunter/jumper shows, but make sure it's dark—leave the one decorated with the crystals at home. At the highest levels of the sport, top hats are customary, though there is no rule against wearing an approved helmet. While we're on the subject, though many dressage riders school without a helmet, I think it's a good idea to wear one whenever you're mounted, no matter what level you're riding.

check box ✓

Take your hand away from the neck when using the whip so you don't interfere too much with the horse's mouth. Always try to tap the horse as close behind your leg as possible, unless you're doing something like a flying change, when you'd touch him farther back, or a piaffe, where you might tap the croup. I hold my whip three inches below the top, but that might not work for you. Just hold it where it feels right, and when you try out whips at the tack shop, select the one whose balance suits you best.

You'll need a flat area where you can work that is laid out in a rectangle and measures at least 20 meters wide and at least two times as long. Don't have anything like that? Just use white jump poles as markers on level ground. When you're starting, you don't need to set down the poles in anything fancier than your regular ring or the field where you do your flatwork at home. As you progress and want to try a dressage test, homemade letters around the ring will do as well as anything you can buy, as long as they're large enough so you can see them clearly. Just copy placement of the letters from the diagrams included later in this book.

AND WHAT ABOUT YOUR HORSE?

Any breed can benefit from dressage training and participate in low-level shows, but if you're going to be a serious contender, you need to consider a horse with a good mind who's a nice mover and has three solid gaits.

I'm not going to tell you how to select a dressage horse. My husband, Bob, is the expert at that, picking all my mounts, and it's a complicated process. Chances are, you'll want to use the horse you already have, whether his previous job experience was in the hunters, jumpers, western pleasure or just going on the trail.

I'll simply offer a few words about what qualities will be helpful in your first dressage horse. It's best to have something that is not built too "downhill"—high behind and short in front—because those horses have a tendency to get heavy on the forehand and can't get their haunches underneath them. That makes it difficult for you to achieve the balance you need to perform the movements properly, though they'll probably be fine for a lower-level dressage test. Ideally, you're looking for a horse that's a little more "uphill," with a front end higher than the back. This type of horse tends to have a freer shoulder and more "reach" with his front legs.

By the way, don't look for a low-traveling "daisy clipper" as you would if you were buying a hunter prospect. You're seeking more elevation in dressage.

A horse that is very wide behind can pose problems, because it is tough to get this conformational type to step under himself. These horses almost start straddling, particularly if they have been pushed too early to have a "big trot."

At the front end, I'd rather have a horse that's too narrow than too wide, because a wide-fronted individual can look irregular in a shoulder-in, since he can't really cross over with his legs. Should he make it as far as piaffe/passage, it might look as if he were swaying from side to side in these movements, so much sometimes it could almost make you seasick!

You should pay attention to the neck, too. Riding a horse with a neck that is too short is almost like driving a Volkswagen bus, as opposed to a limousine with a long front, because he'll have trouble stretching down and using his back properly. Basically, a short neck is just not as good a look as a horse with a longer neck. But even worse is a horse with an upside-down or ewe neck, because it will be very hard to get him on the bit. An optimum neck would come out of the

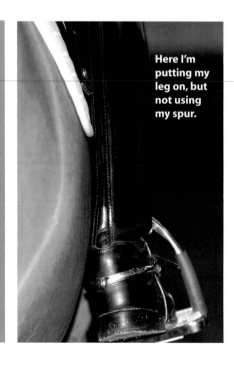

check box

Every person's leg will hang differently according to the length of leg. My leg is not very long, which means it's obstructed by the belly of the horse. Even if your leg is longer, where the leg hangs a little more around the bottom of the barrel, remember that the leg is not supposed to be "on" continually while you're riding. You keep the leg relaxed and soft. If putting the leg on gets no results, that is when you use the spur.

Here I'm putting my leg on, but not using my spur.

I don't want you to be discouraged should your horse's conformation or gaits not be perfect.
Try to work with what you have if it's not possible to get a better candidate for dressage,
because there is much you can learn even if you never go to a show.

shoulders in an arched way. Yet there's another caveat here—a neck that is too long could cause a problem getting the horse on the aids if the poll is not the highest point.

You should also take your horse's mouth into account. You want a horse that is quiet in the mouth. That means the horse isn't messing with the bit and showing his teeth.

Some horses have tongue issues and pain that stem from a variety of causes, from an improperly fitted bit to a rider's bad hands and lack of a good connection. A good connection, when you develop it, can fix most mouth problems. If a horse isn't foaming in the mouth, that usually means the connection isn't good. We've found, strangely enough, that some horses with tongue issues are not comfortable in their hocks.

It goes without saying that if there's a mouth problem, you need to have a dentist look at your horse, and attend to the teeth at least once a year, if not more often. Some horses are just plain oral and want to be constantly trying to open their mouths.

No horse is going to be perfect all the way around, but the ideal is a well-balanced horse whose walk has four distinct beats. On a free (loose) rein, a horse should have an overstep, meaning the hind foot steps over the front hoofprint. If a horse has a good walk, he usually has a good canter. Conversely, if one is bad, so is the other, and they're both tough to fix. The canter needs to be three beats, and the optimum is for the hind leg to step under the rider's seat. The trot, which has a two-beat rhythm, can be improved upon with patience and proper guidance.

Let me give you one more idea. A schoolmaster, an experienced horse that is in semi-retirement or is not able to compete at the highest levels anymore because of age or soundness issues, can be a marvelous teacher. Even if you don't own this horse, leasing him or taking lessons on him will benefit you enormously if you can go that route. It's nice to have a horse that can train you.

Once you have the basics—the right tack, somewhere to work and a horse that is willing, you're ready to learn dressage. So let's go!

A long leg hanging in the relaxed position.

My short leg is close to the horse's barrel, which makes it easy to use the spur.

To test self-carriage, give a moment on the inside rein and see if the horse can still maintain the balance and rhythm.

CHAPTER 3

Perfecting the Basics

THERE ARE A NUMBER OF PRINCIPLES YOU MUST UNDERSTAND TO SUCCEED in dressage. Consider them the building blocks required to start going up the levels of the sport. Take whatever time is necessary to learn a correct halt, half-halt and transitions between the walk, trot and canter. Done properly, they will provide a firm foundation for whatever your goal may be, whether it's constructing a good framework for a well-done First Level test, or putting together the platform for a towering achievement, such as competing at Grand Prix. Skipping a step, or going to the next step before perfecting the last, can only result in disappointment.

Some mistakes are tough to fix; you can't just start again once the damage has been done. That's why I believe in keeping the training simple enough so the horse always knows what you want. From the very beginning, that means sensitivity to the aids—your legs, seat, hands and voice. When you apply your leg, the horse must respond by going forward; no excuses. If your horse does not respond to the aids, you will run into problems and wind up at a dead end. Until your horse is reacting promptly to the aids, you shouldn't go to the next step in your work.

Do not make a horse feel pushed or stressed in his work. My horses work 30 minutes a day, five days a week, with longeing, turnout, time on a walker or a combination of all three on the off-days. I've never had a horse come out of his stall sore from the previous day's work.

Allow each horse to learn at his own pace. Some 4-year-olds will be able to do what certain 6-year-olds can't do. There are gifted horses, just as there are gifted people. You have to listen to your horse in order to keep the work at the right level. Learn one thing at a time, and learn it well.

Before we get going, here are some things to keep in mind to make sure the work goes well:

- **Develop sensitivity to the aids.**
- **Allow each horse to learn at his own pace.**
- **Keep the training simple enough so the horse always knows what you want.**
- **There is no substitute for a good seat and independent aids.**

check box ✔

Although this book will educate you about the basics of dressage and help you through some training issues, there is no substitute for having a good instructor. This is especially helpful as you try to establish your seat and position. From there, the trainer also can evaluate the progress that you and your horse are making, which is particularly important if you do not have the experience to judge for yourself by looking in a mirror as you ride.

This is a good demonstration of a horse nicely on the bit.

I will say one more time before we get started: **There is no substitute for a good seat and independent aids!** You should do everything in your power to seek good help to get things started on the right foot.

LONG AND LOW

I always start my rides with the horse long and low, and finish work the same way.

Riding long and low, with an open angle between the neck and head as the horse stretches toward the ground, is an excellent technique to reward him after hard work. It also stretches the neck muscles and back, which eventually will enable the horse to carry himself in a better frame.

*How do you get the horse to accept the bit? You do it by riding him through lots of transitions,
asking him to be sensitive to the aids. When the horse is correctly on the bit, it doesn't require a lot of leg
to keep him there. The horse should be moving forward willingly into a calm, even connection,
and always follow the contact, using only the amount of rein you are giving.*

To get the horse to go long and low, push him into the bit and then gradually ease off with your hands, allowing him to chew the bit and take the reins from you gently. Don't let him yank the reins.

If a horse is reluctant to go long and low, you should take up on the reins to get a better connection. When the horse has a good connection, he should be more than willing to stretch when asked.

I pay attention to the rhythm and make sure the horse is still adjustable in it. If I take a little feel and ask the horse to come back and he does not, then I know he is running a bit on the forehand instead of properly stretching his muscles and topline. In that moment, I will take him up again and work on the connection. As I've said before, if the connection is not right, chances are that the stretching will not be right, either.

I like to do some transitions from trot to walk, walk to trot and trot to canter so I know that the horse is truly through, connected from back to front, and relaxed in his back before I pick him up and continue with my work.

As you go along, make the work fun. If you think the horse has done something really well, get into jumping position off his back and canter forward. Let him feel as if he's galloping (but don't let him get out of control, of course).

Remember, though, the horse needs to be correctly on the aids at all times when you are on his back. Where that begins is with walk-halt transitions.

On the Bit

On the bit is an often-used term, but it can be misleading, as some may think it means the horse should be leaning on the bit. Actually, what we are talking about when we say "on the bit" is an acceptance of the bit.

This is indicated by the horse carrying his neck in an arched position slightly in front of the vertical, with the poll being the highest point. To find the vertical, draw a straight line from the forelock to the nose. There should be a soft and equal contact in both reins, with no tilting or twisting of the head. Although "on the bit" sounds as if it only applies to the horse's mouth, it in fact involves the horse's entire body and his way of carrying himself.

For a horse to be truly "on the bit," we must think of the process as starting from the hind end. The horse's hind legs should be stepping under his body and carrying weight equally, enabling the front end of the horse (and therefore the contact) to become lighter and softer.

The horse's back and neck should be supple, and he should not be leaning on the reins or hollowing his back. When the horse carries himself with this suppleness and balance, the rider will feel the horse's neck softly arching out in front of him, and there is always a slight feeling that the horse is ready and willing to stretch to the contact.

When the horse is correctly on the bit, he will carry it quietly in his mouth. He may softly chew it, but his mouth will not be open and chomping excessively. Getting a horse on the bit involves the balance and suppleness of the horse's whole body and cannot be accomplished by simply pulling a horse's head around.

The contact never should be fatiguing. You should not feel as if you are dealing with a pressure that is not comfortable to hold in your hand. You will increase the engagement—how much the hind end carries—as you go up through the levels, and the elevation of the horse's head will rise along the way.

The horse must answer the hand as well as the leg. A lot of people get caught up with running their horses forward, but still don't have the "whoa." It's not about running the horse off his feet, as happens in too many warm-ups, but rather about teaching him a rhythm through a good connection and half-halts.

Here Dolce, who is only four years old, is completely relaxed and stretching to the bit as Adrienne warms her up.

HALTS

The transitions you'll be making with your horse that are detailed in this chapter are in reality teaching half-halts; that is, asking your horse to wait and rebalance for a moment before continuing in the gait. The half-halt is a tool you'll develop throughout his training as you educate him to carry himself better. At the higher levels of dressage, this adds impulsion and expression to any gait or movement.

Halting from the walk can be more difficult than halting from the trot or canter, because there is no impulsion in the walk, which means there is no thrust into a period of suspension. But you have to master the halt at the walk before

check box ✓

If I have a horse who is reluctant to stretch, I will do some leg-yields (see page 43) at the walk, bringing him back and asking him to walk on. Even in the walk, trying to get the horse to give in his back is helpful. Sometimes it is easier to start with a few steps of medium walk, then ask the horse to walk out almost to a free walk. If the horse will not take up the slack in the reins when I ask him to move on, I will repeat the exercise until he does. I make that my goal for the day. Do the same at the trot and it will improve the horse's connection.

I will say that there are a few horses who are a bit more complicated than this and require a different type of warm-up, with not as much stretching. There are horses I have been given to train that are impossible to bring back up if you start them long and low. Even though I feel horses in the latter category are few and far between, I must at least mention that you need to be open-minded when working with horses and treat them all as individuals.

**Here the rider has
achieved a square halt.**

*It's important that the horse learns he has to execute a square halt. Every time I dismount,
I like to have my horse stand square, so it becomes a no-brainer for him—he learns to
square up automatically when he halts. Following that procedure means there's
one less thing you have to worry about in the arena.*

you try it from the trot. Although I'm addressing a lot of the beginning work through walk/halt, the end product of what we're looking for in dressage is a horse who's willingly moving ahead with a nice, light connection. You have to go with your horse, allowing him to develop his full range of motion, rather than restricting him. So

when you address the walk/halt, make sure the horse doesn't become afraid of your hand. If you want a horse who's sensitive in the mouth, you can't start hauling on him. Softening your hand should become a reward, especially if a horse is green and has no idea what you mean when you ask for the halt.

**Keep your reins
in each hand when you
pat your horse.**

Remember that working with every horse requires repetition and patience.

Be aware you can't expect too much from a young horse or one that is just starting to be trained. Don't drill them; we're trying to get our horses to enjoy their work.

To begin, close your fingers and add a little bit of resistance in the horse's mouth. Don't close your leg in the same way as if you're asking the horse to go forward. The way your legs lie on the horse's body should instead give him more of a secure feeling, almost like a gentle hug. Just squeeze a little with your thighs, sit up straighter to brace yourself, and block any forward motion from the horse with your hands.

How much hand pressure you need in asking for the halt depends on the horse. Although we want the end product to be the same for all horses, every horse reacts differently in that regard, so you have to get to know yours and what works for him. Listen to what the horse is trying to tell you. This is something that will be important all through your partnership, and you should eventually be able to have quite a dialogue with your horse, learning how to communicate through your aids.

When you get what you're looking for, reward the horse immediately, lightening the connection as soon as he halts and patting him to let him know that halt was exactly what you wanted. I always try to pat my horse on the inside of his neck (with the hand toward the center of the arena), so I can continue to support him with the outside rein. Move your hand forward to give just a quick pat, then bring it right back. Don't let the reins droop too much, or put all your reins in the outside hand, because that will disrupt your connection.

I've never ridden a horse who didn't react in a good way when I patted him. On certain issues and with major achievements, I'll make an even bigger deal of it, speaking with more enthusiasm at a little higher pitch than normal, saying "Yes!" or "Good boy!" to let him know he's on track. Not everyone uses voice, but I like it, because it gives me an extra tool, so to speak. I always remind my students, however, not to use voice in competition, since that's against the rules. So be careful that you don't completely rely on your voice as an aid. It can, however, be useful in certain situations, as I'll explain later.

Your initial walk/halt work involves developing a response to the aids, the "whoa" and the "go." Once you've established that, it's time for the next step, refining the halt. It's important during this process that you listen closely to your horse. If you feel he's getting frustrated with this exercise, let him move forward by going to the posting (also called rising) trot and "escaping" for a few moments.

Never make a horse feel trapped by your demands on him. Before you attempt to perfect the halt, make sure the horse is comfortable just standing there, even if his legs aren't perfectly aligned. Don't attempt to square him up until you're sure he doesn't fear standing quietly in the arena for a few seconds.

check box ✓

If you have a horse who's tough in the mouth and doesn't want to halt, or has a tendency to throw his head up in the air at these moments, try flexing him to one side or the other as you ask for the halt, while "playing the bit" by gently moving your fingers to make the bit lively in his mouth for a moment. Just make sure you have a good connection (that is, you're not doing it on a loose rein, and making sure you have a feel of both sides of the horse's mouth, even when flexing slightly). Don't take his head too strongly to either side. You're not supposed to be wagging the head by pulling the bit through the mouth; this is a subtle movement. What you're saying is, "Hey, pay attention." Playing the bit, also called shaking the bit, is a technique I use quite a lot, and one that can work just as well for you.

Your halt must be square, with the horse's front legs and back legs parallel to each other. A halt like this, where the left hind is so far back, will lose you points in a dressage test.

A gentle tap with the whip on the offending leg will tell your horse to move it forward so you can square him up.

When I'm teaching my horses, I do my halts sideways to the mirror in the indoor arena so I can see all four legs. If you don't have a mirror, you need someone on the ground to watch what's going on. In this case, your helper doesn't have to be an expert; she just has to tell you how the horse is standing.

The horse should always square up in a forward way, that is, by stepping ahead and under his body. You don't want him to step back to square up. You'll get a lower mark in your dressage tests for that.

Most horses have a tendency to keep one hind leg back, and you have to correct that. Here's how to do it: If this continually happens with the left hind, for instance, I'll put the whip on the left side. When we halt, if I look in the mirror and see my horse is not squaring up, I'll immediately tap him lightly behind my leg to get him to move the leg forward. Don't tap too hard—after all, you have told the horse to halt.

If the horse moves the leg forward, even if he's not quite square yet, I'll reward him to let him know he's on the right track. I also may add a quiet little cluck that I can use as a subtle signal to square up, even in the ring, since the judge wouldn't be able to hear it.

A square halt is vital in competition. When you stop and salute in a test, the horse must be immobile, though there is no set time that you need to stand still. While you're training, however, you should halt for longer than you would in front of a judge. Your horse

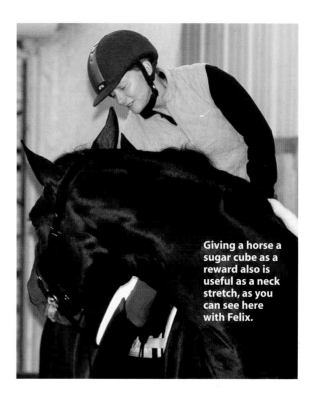

Giving a horse a sugar cube as a reward also is useful as a neck stretch, as you can see here with Felix.

needs to be comfortable in the halt. If he tends to get stressed, I'd make the stop time shorter at first. Don't force the horse to stand there until he gets crazed and afraid of the halt.

Horses have to learn to enjoy the halt, and know there's nothing to be afraid of, that it's actually a nice break. Sometimes, in training, I'll even give them a sugar cube. I don't do it every time I halt, though, and I would never give it to them if they asked for it without my offering it. The horse needs to wait until it is given.

check box ✓

The outside rein is what enables you to control the amount of flexion and bend for lateral movements. Flexion, used to supple the horse through the poll, is a slight positioning of the head to either side, which does not involve the neck. Bend involves not only the neck, but also curving the horse's entire body around either of the rider's legs. Too little outside rein, and your horse will overbend as you hang on the inside rein. Too much outside rein, and the horse can't bend. Don't forget to use your legs in conjunction with the reins. The aids must be independent but coordinated. The amount of bend for every movement is slightly different, and also depends on what level you're riding. As a general rule, though, the degree of bend in the horse's neck is a continuum of the degree of bend in his body. If you're looking for a quick check, stick with the tried and true axiom—when your horse is bent, you should just be able to see the corner of his eye. Any more, and he's probably overbent.

The principle is the same one I use when I ask a horse to stretch down; he shouldn't be seeking more rein than I'm giving. Of course, I don't offer sugar as a reward in the warm-up for a class, because that could cause a problem during my test if he suddenly decides he wants another treat.

HALF-HALT

I start teaching my young horses the half-halt early in their training, because it is so crucial in balance and transitions. I use a lot of halt/walk transitions in a warm-up as a barometer of my horse's degree of readiness, and to determine whether he's listening to me before I go on with the rest of our work. How do you know whether your horse is listening? Does he respond immediately when you ask him to halt or move forward? If the answer is yes, then he's paying attention.

To do a half-halt, start with a simple walk, then halt and praise the horse. Once this process is clear in the horse's mind, start walking, come almost to the halt, release and walk on, trying not to disrupt the rhythm of the gait.

As you go into the half-halt, brace a little with your seat and back, then close your fingers, making a strong fist. It might be necessary to lock the elbow for a couple of seconds to give a slight resistance. If you hold the resistance too long and do not support with your leg, the horse will break. So keep your legs at the horse's sides, supporting (not driving, which would ask the horse to go forward). This should condense the energy, not stifle it. Be careful that the horse doesn't "stall"; make sure you don't lose the tempo!

When you've got it at the walk, try it at the trot, but instead of coming almost to halt, you would come almost to the walk. In the canter, you would come almost to the trot. Be patient. Half-halt is something that needs to be practiced in order for a horse to truly understand what you want. But in every gait, remember that you must keep the energy through the half-halt and channel it as the horse moves forward again.

WALK AND TROT

Make sure the horse is responsive to the upward transition. If you close your leg for the trot and "nobody's home," use both legs more forcefully, bumping him with your calves (but being careful not to stick him with your spurs). Don't hold a grudge. Discipline your horse and move on. Continue to be consistent with your aids until it gets to the point where just thinking "trot" should make it happen.

The horse must stay connected throughout your walk/trot/halt transitions. If you halt and your horse starts looking around, that's the moment that I would move him on, but then you need to come back and school the exercise some more so he learns to connect into the contact, back to front. Think, "Use the leg before the hand, not the hand before the leg."

It can become a huge issue if he comes off the bit in the arena to go "sightseeing." If you have to take time in front of the judges to get him back on the bit, you've already lost points as your test is beginning, and it can be an equally bad note on which to finish your ride.

This leads me to another point: **Your horse has to go with the rein length you choose to carry, not the one he selects.** This is not an argument you can afford to lose. If the horse throws his head upside down in training because he doesn't want you to hold it, then walk circles or do leg-yields to get him to come back in the frame and go on the outside rein.

Don't put on too much pressure with your legs

check box ✓

What if things go wrong? If you're unbalanced, or something's not working, come back to a place in your work where you feel confident that you can get your point across to re-establish your connection with the horse. Then think about your problem, asking yourself, "Why isn't it working?" The answer may be, "because the horse is not listening to my leg," or "because he's too strong in my hand." You have to learn to become a thinking rider, to dissect what has gone wrong and then figure out how to fix it. Don't just react; think first.

when you ask for the walk or the horse will get lateral and travel like a camel, where the legs on the same side move together, instead of in a proper four-beat gait. In that situation, there will be tension in the walk. That's why I will circle while pushing the horse with my inside leg toward the outside rein, urging him to step slightly sideways. When there's tension involved in the walk, going in straight lines promotes more lateral tendencies—which is something horses with a "big" walk are prone to anyway.

I don't do a lot of walking on a straight line with much in the way of collection until the horse learns to accept the contact and step up through the hand. Once the horse accepts contact, I can regulate the walk through half-halting and releasing. What does that mean? When you close your fingers more firmly on the reins, the horse needs to come back with a shorter step but doesn't change tempo. If he doesn't do that, he's running through your hand. That's where lateral tendencies start, as the horse gets quicker and begins to lean, almost using your hands as a fifth leg, rather than coming back when you ask.

It's all about adjustability. You have to be able to control the tempo and the length of your horse's steps.

To shorten in the trot, bring your horse back in the same manner as if you were going to come down to a walk, until you feel the trot start to shorten. You have your legs on the horse to provide energy, so you're telling the horse he can't walk, but your hands warn him he can't trot too fast; he has to stay within the boundaries you set. When you've reached the trot you desire—and it has to be the trot you choose, not the trot the horse chooses—don't hang on the reins. If he starts to run the moment you ease up, drop back to the walk and halt, making your point with your hands as to what you want him to do. When you have him listening to you, go forward in the normal sitting trot and ask the horse to shorten again. Do this until you feel the horse is waiting for your command and stays under your seat, rather than relying on the hand to keep him in that short trot. Little half-halts, rather than one strong pull, should keep him where you want him.

Lengthening in the trot is exactly what it says:

a longer step at that gait, rather than a faster, shorter step.

Start in a rising trot. Close your leg, then slightly soften your hands on the reins, which encourages the horse to move into the bit and take up any slack. If the horse isn't taking you across the arena willingly and you have to push him, you'll find you're getting a short, choppy stride.

To fix that, instead of trying to push-push-push and go bigger, I will take the horse back, tapping the whip on his side behind my leg a couple of times, encouraging him to move forward and be more sensitive to my leg.

check box ✓

Many times I've taught people who say about their horse, "He's doing this" or "He's doing that," whether he's constantly picking up the wrong lead or isn't listening to the leg. And I say, "You're absolutely right. But who's going to fix it?" By that, I mean it's up to the rider. It does no good to just complain about a problem—it's your job to analyze the situation, think of a remedy and take action.

Then I try again for the lengthening. If necessary, I will repeat the process until the horse takes me to the other end of the arena without effort on my part.

Should the horse go faster than I've asked him to and I can't get him to react by simply closing my fingers, I use more hand to bring him back and play the bit to get his attention. If the horse goes faster than I want him to, however, and I don't correct him, it's the start of a bad habit. You must stay alert to monitor every footfall, and act immediately if your horse isn't obeying your commands.

THE CANTER

Let's say we have a young horse just learning canter transitions. The main thing you want to do (and actually, this applies to any horse) is to break it down to his level.

Take a break from work with a trail ride to keep you and your horse fresh.

Don't make the mistake of thinking that just because we believe something is easy that it is going to be easy for the horse. You always want to set him up for success, not failure, so you must plan carefully to make sure you don't over-face your mount.

If you have jumping experience, you realize you don't take a horse who has never cleared anything higher than 3 feet and put him in front of a 5-foot oxer, expecting him to leap it gracefully (or at all!). You must build up to every task you require of your horse.

When you know you've got your trot/walk and walk/trot transitions down pat and you're finally ready to start cantering, begin with a 20-meter circle at the trot at one end of the arena. That way, you have three

until I feel in the upward transition that the horse is reacting promptly, reaching toward the bit and staying nicely connected in both reins. When I've got all that, I will half-halt so the horse doesn't run faster when I apply my aids. Then I move my inside leg a little forward, and take my outside leg back slightly, squeezing with both legs at the same time. You've got to make sure that you don't throw the horse off balance, and that he reacts to your legs.

If the horse executes that transition correctly, I praise him, even if he got playful in the process. I'm not worrying about that at the moment. All I'm expecting is that the horse wants to go into the canter and picks up the correct lead.

*Don't forget: It's all about connection, balance and sensitivity to the aids, as well as
the rider's attention to asking the horse for transitions at the right moment.*

sides of your circle against the wall. When you are on the open side of the circle, approaching the rail, think about making your transition into the canter. You're coming up on a wall, so you've got to keep turning in that direction, guiding with the inside rein. Keep following the line of the circle, while checking that you have kept a good connection on the outside rein. How do you know you have it? When you feel you could give a moment on the inside rein and the horse can still maintain balance and rhythm, you've got it.

At the moment of transition, you will have slightly more weight in your outside rein, which will help keep control of the outside shoulder. Your inside rein will be guiding the horse in the direction you are going. It's very important to let the inside shoulder stay open, so it can come up and into the proper lead. If you're holding too tightly on the inside, you're stopping the horse's inside leg from stepping through. That will make him feel a little bit trapped, and could hamper his ability to pick up the canter on the correct lead.

Before going into a canter I like to do some tempo changes in the trot. I ask the horse to go forward and backward, making sure he is quick off my leg. I do that

If he tries to run off or throws his head up too much, cut him a little slack as he feels his way through to getting balanced. Don't be too quick to get after the horse at that time. I would just try to make the transition a little cleaner through patience. The horse must truly understand there's nothing for him to fear, if it's one of the first times he has done this with a person on his back. He's going to feel very awkward, and need time to develop through proper practice.

If you're not successful in getting the canter transition at all and the horse just trots faster, bring him back in the trot, working on his sensitivity to the aids with a few forward-and-back strides before asking again.

Still unsuccessful? Then carry a little whip on the outside. The horse is going to move away from the whip, not into the whip. So if you want the left lead, put the whip in your right hand. Tap the horse lightly behind your leg and be prepared for him to be a little playful, making sure you're sitting securely in the middle of your saddle. Be careful not to grab the horse in the mouth in that crucial moment; that would be punishing him for doing what you asked him to do.

Once you get the canter, continue in that gait until

I love this picture because it shows a happy four-year-old mare enjoying what she is doing. The canter demonstrates good engagement of a horse nicely on the bit.

the horse has established a few strides and he understands what you want, before you bring him back to the trot and pat him.

If he picks up the wrong lead, bring the horse back to a controlled trot. Take a moment to make him sensitive to your leg, bumping him with it and flexing him briefly to the outside before trying again. Picking up the wrong lead means the horse is out of balance. Are your reins even? More than likely, he ran through the outside shoulder. So much of picking up the canter is also timing and feel of the rider—the mistake is not always the horse's fault.

While I apply a little pressure with the outside leg when I'm signaling the horse to canter, I make sure he is also aware of my inside leg. The reason I do this is because in other movements you've taught the horse to move **away** from the leg. So if you only apply the outside leg or you apply it too strongly, he'll swing away from it in the flying change when he's supposed to be straight. Over the years of training horses to do flying changes, I've found the most successful straight flying changes are from horses very sensitive to lighter aids. So the best thing to do is sit quietly, rather than throwing your body from side to side. Sometimes you'll see a rider doing better changes than the horse! A rider who throws herself around in the saddle for the changes causes the horse to swing a lot. The way to fix that is by training the horse to react to lighter/sensitive aids.

You may not be thinking about flying changes when you're working on getting a horse to take a few canter strides for the first time, but remember you're planting a seed that will bloom and grow over the years. I've found that if you teach them this way from the very beginning, it makes the learning process so much easier later, when you are actually ready to do the flying changes.

But back to the early stages, once I know the horse understands the transition into the

Giving Your Horse Confidence in You

If you want to have a relationship with your horse, you have to know him at all times, not just when you're on his back. You have to recognize his quirks, how he stands and how he sleeps. Some horses like to stand with one leg cocked. If you know that horse, you'll recognize that it's a pattern, rather than a problem.

I spend as much time as I can with my horses when I'm in the barn. I call them all by their names. I give them lots of treats and scratch them, or kiss them on the nose. If I'm home in Idaho on a day off, you'll often see me at the barn clipping their legs or giving them a bath. I do all that stuff. To me, that's the whole package. I don't think you can just get on a horse and expect him to perform for you if he has no love for you. Sure, for the most part they try to please, but will there be that extra little something in the relationship? I don't think so. You have to put the effort in if you expect to get the effort out.

It's very important for your horse to recognize your voice. If you were to go into a large crowd of people and they're making lots of noise and that horse has a terrified look on his face, you could be in trouble. When the fans greet Brentina as we're trotting into the arena at a big event like the World Cup finals or the Olympics, I can feel her saying, "Oh, do I need to be nervous here?" And I say, "It's okay, you're fine. They're all here for you!"

But there's a long-term basis for being able to have that type of quick fix in an adrenaline moment. I have let Brentina know over the years that I would never put her in a situation where she'd have to worry, ever. I would never try to do anything with her I didn't know she could do.

With your own horse, you may get in trouble when you start doing a movement at a stage that's too early for a horse's development. If you pressure that kind of issue with a horse and start beating on him to get it done, you've lost the horse's confidence. I'm not saying you can't discipline him properly, but you have to recognize when the horse is capable of learning that next step before you start asking for it, because that horse has to believe in you.

canter, then I start trying to focus on the quality of the gait. That means teaching the horse how to be supple, balanced and straight, making sure he isn't "popping" the outside shoulder. Often, a young horse needs help teaching him to be straight. Most of the time, the haunches lean to the inside and the shoulder falls, or "pops," out. Lots of riders try to correct the haunches, but the crux of the problem is that the shoulder is falling to the outside because they no longer have a real connection on the outside rein. The rider often hangs on the inside rein, instead of making the horse stand up and get off his outside shoulder.

You can fix that with a slight counter-flexion to the outside, just enough to make sure the horse is giving in the poll and that he's not tight in the neck or strong in the mouth. Hold the flexion there for a moment, and then soften the contact. Sometimes you have to do it several times. If it doesn't seem as if he's getting the picture, use a little outside leg to prevent him from leaning too much on the outside shoulder.

Early on, after I know the horse is trying to carry himself, without using my hands as his fifth leg, I work on changes in tempo and length of stride. I do a few strides of lengthening and a few strides of working canter. The minute the horse comes back to me, I reward him with a quick pat.

TURN ON THE FOREHAND

I don't use the turn on the forehand very often, but I know it is something that many people like to have in their tool box, even though it's not part of any dressage test.

If you've done a bit of riding, chances are you're already familiar with the turn on the forehand. The purpose of this movement is to help the horse loosen his hindquarters and teach him to move away from the pushing aids. The rider should make sure that the flexion is away from the direction in which the horse is moving, just as in a leg-yield. The horse should cross his back legs as he moves around the front legs, which stay almost on the same spot during the movement.

When doing this, make sure that you do not bend the horse's neck too much; it should be just a flexion. Otherwise, the movement will become more of a leg-yield, with back and front legs crossing.

THE REIN-BACK

When I know that the horse understands and isn't afraid of the halt and the connection, I start to address a few steps of rein-back (backing up).

I do my initial work from the ground. Facing the bridled horse, I put my left hand on the right rein and my right hand on the left rein. Because my body is blocking his forward progress, the horse may be more willing to

Remember, when a horse is correctly into both reins, it should feel as if you could momentarily "give" both reins forward and the horse would remain in the same rhythm and tempo.

Once the horse really understands the aid for canter from the trot, try it from the walk. Again, you want to make sure you're not hanging on the inside rein. If you feel the horse is not even in both reins, you should do more forward and back transitions, going from the walk into the trot and back to the walk, until the connection is even. Remember when a horse is correctly into both reins it should feel as if you could momentarily "give" both reins forward and the horse would remain in the same rhythm and tempo.

step backwards. Sometimes I'll have an assistant stand with me and put light pressure on the horse's chest with a hand while I keep holding the reins. What you're looking for is a horse who reacts to what you want him to do in a non-fearful way.

If these techniques aren't successful, I'd have the person standing in front of me tap the horse gently on the chest or coronary band with a whip, so he gets the idea of going backward. I have known horses to get more fearful with pressure and in that instance, I have used a treat

*Right from the start, though, I have to tell you that dressage is not
a sport you should take up if you are not interested in staying focused
the entire time you're sitting on a horse's back.*

---

held in the palm of my hand at the level of the horse's chest. In order to get it, he'll have to reach for it and in effect be getting a reward as he steps backward himself. Say the word "Back," repeatedly as you train him. That is a verbal tool you can use for emphasis when you try to back up the horse while you are mounted.

To work on the rein-back once I'm in the saddle, I start from a halt, with equal contact in both reins. Next, I ask the horse to step back using a small amount of resistance in the rein while I bring both of my lower legs back a little, to give him the idea of backward.

When I get one step from a horse, I'll reward it, even if it's crooked, as long as the horse is willing to step backward. After I pat him, I give him another reward by letting him walk forward.

If your horse is resistant in the rein-back and braces, in effect saying, "I'm not going to go backward," don't lose your cool. I've seen far too many instances where the rider becomes impatient with the horse. At that point, the horse really becomes fearful of the rein-back, throwing his head up and, in a worst-case scenario, rearing. Horses naturally don't like to back up, because they can't see behind them. They need a lot of confidence in the rider to back up, and that's what you've been working on developing. You'll keep on perfecting the rein-back throughout your early training period with your horse; don't try to do it all in just a few sessions.

DON'T LET YOUR HORSE TRAIN YOU

During this phase of your developing partnership with your horse, you must address issues as they come up. Little issues become big issues when you put off dealing with problems, thinking, "I'll fix it later."

Some people who have a horse with a little bit of a spooky streak try to run through a problem area as fast as they can, which leads to havoc. If my horse spooks at the trot or canter, I'll work through the problem slowly by immediately coming back to the walk, where I know he can't get away from me. That's important: As I've said before, never let the horse think that he's calling the shots. We always say around our barn, "Don't let your horse train you."

Allowing him to do so can quickly crumble the foundation that you have labored to build. But if your horse has confidence in you (see box on page 39), together you can overcome nearly any problem you encounter.

I hope all of this doesn't sound overwhelming, since we've only just begun. Right from the start, though, I have to tell you that dressage is not a sport you should take up if you are not interested in staying focused the entire time you're sitting on a horse's back. There has to be constant communication, and that requires concentration.

If you want to think about your love life or the office, go on a trail ride that day. In the arena, your job is to keep your horse connected from back to front, which is what **riding through** is all about. It's a constant communication between horse and rider. When you're connected, everything looks easy. The horse can go from one movement to the next without changing the rhythm or being stressed. You should feel as if the horse is willing to stretch down and forward into the contact at any time, even if you're not asking for it at a certain moment. The horse needs to stay supple and loose in the back.

Here's a leg-yield being done correctly; Adrienne is looking toward where she is going. Her horse, Miguel, is looking in the other direction.

CHAPTER 4

Moving On Up

WHEN YOU FEEL YOUR HORSE IS DOING WALK-TROT-CANTER AND HALT transitions well, he's ready to start developing the lateral (sideways) movements, starting with leg-yields, shoulder-in, travers (haunches-in), renvers (haunches-out) and half-pass—but not all in the same day! Lateral work teaches a horse to be more supple and truly on the aids. It also helps develop more collection, which will be helpful in moving on up the levels.

LEG-YIELD

Before a horse can do a shoulder-in, he has to know what a leg-yield is. If you're looking for a quick reference or refresher on any of these movements, you can find them easily in the "recipes" in Chapter 6, page 61.

Bear in mind that when you are starting any of the movements, you want the horse to know what direction he's going. In the case of the leg-yield, instead of keeping the horse completely parallel to the rail and pushing him over toward the wall, I'll begin gradually.

Start by coming off a left turn on a diagonal line. As you approach the centerline, begin applying your right leg to ask him to step sideways to the left, keeping him slightly flexed toward your right leg, the one he is moving away from. You should feel as if you could almost let go of the right rein because he'll be so much on the outside rein that he's yielding to your leg and heading where he's supposed to go. In whatever direction you do your leg-yield, make sure your outside rein is slightly away from the neck so the horse steps over to it. Your inside rein should be close to the neck and supporting, but don't cross the neck with it. As you continue, stay on the diagonal to keep the quality of the gait, rather than just focusing on going sideways. This approach simplifies in the horse's mind the direction in which he should be going, because he's already moving that way off the turn. It's a given that the horse is moving **away from** the inside leg in the leg-yield.

check box ✔

There is no rule saying you have to stay at a certain point for so many days, or weeks. Make sure the horse knows what you want and consistently does it at your command. Then you can move on.

In this chapter, you'll learn about:

■ **Lateral movements, the key to a more supple horse and moving up the levels**

I'll take you through:

■ **The leg-yield**

■ **Shoulder-in**

■ **Haunches-in**

■ **Haunches-out**

■ **Half-pass**

You'll get an idea of when you and your horse should move up. We'll also discuss maintaining the quality of the gaits while you do this work. That's important as you develop a horse who is naturally relaxed in his back and moves freely forward in the contact.

Leg-Yield Diagram 1

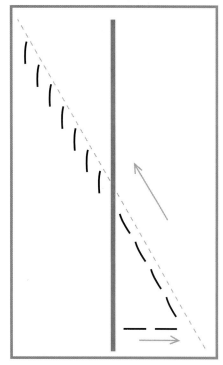

Leg-Yield Diagram 2

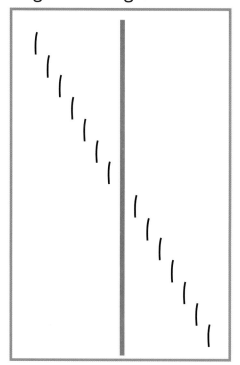

As I'm turning, I don't completely straighten the horse. I've already given him a place to go with his shoulder, and with my inside leg, I urge the horse to move his haunches over and complete the movement (see leg-yield diagram 1).

When he knows what I'm asking, I make it a little more difficult, so eventually I can start a leg-yield when I'm parallel to the wall (see leg-yield diagram 2).

You've got a good leg-yield when the horse is parallel to the wall, with haunches and shoulders both meeting it at the same time, never losing the quality of the trot and moving forward and sideways. The haunches should never reach the wall before the shoulder.

But don't be discouraged if it takes you a while to reach that point. Once the horse can keep his normal working trot and carry that rhythm sideways, it's correct.

SHOULDER-IN

To begin the shoulder-in at the walk, execute a 10-meter circle with your inside leg at the girth and your outside leg just behind the girth, ensuring the haunches don't fall out, which would make it a leg-yield. As you approach the rail, at the place where you would start your circle over

again (you almost want the horse to think he's continuing on the circle), half-halt, making sure your outside rein is connected, or the shoulder will fall back to the rail. Using your inside lower leg, ask the horse to go down the long side of the arena with his shoulders slightly off the track as you look forward down the rail. The inside rein helps guide the horse's shoulders off the rail, providing flexion; the outside rein steadies him. The outside leg ensures the horse doesn't throw the haunches to the outside; the inside leg maintains the forward motion and the horse's bend, which should be even from head to tail as the horse steps along on three tracks.

check box ✓

You know you are putting too much emphasis on the sideways part of the leg-yield when you lose the rhythm and cadence in your trot and you feel stuck. The horse should always feel as if he's taking you to the end of the arena, not like you're pushing him.

How long should you do the leg-yield before moving on to the shoulder-in and eventually the haunches-in? Until the horse really understands the concept of moving away from your leg and stepping into the outside rein.

Hoof Position Diagram

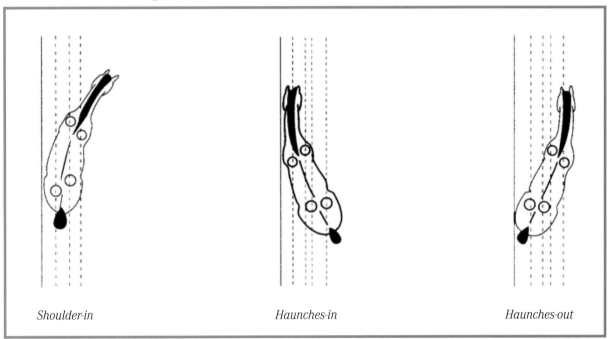

Shoulder-in	*Haunches-in*	*Haunches-out*

When the horse understands the leg-yield and shoulder-in, the rest of the lateral work at the trot is not very difficult.

HAUNCHES-IN

After you are comfortable with what the shoulder-in feels like, you're ready to move on to the next step, the haunches-in, or travers (pronounced: tra-vayr).

I like to start this movement by riding along the short side of the arena. I cut the corner slightly, so the haunches do not reach the rail, half-halt and move my outside leg behind the girth. I am going to ask my horse to do a leg-yield facing the wall. This way, the wall on the long side of the ring does a lot of the work for you, keeping the horse from running forward while he's moving away from your outside leg with the haunches off the track to the inside. Eventually, you're aiming to have the haunches at the same angle off the rail as you did with the shoulders in the shoulder-in. The goal, as with the shoulder-in, is to have the horse on three tracks.

After that, rather than just continuing with a leg-yield against the wall, teach the horse to bend his body in the direction of travel around your new inside leg. When the horse gives at all to the flexing rein, reward him by returning to the leg-yield facing the wall, just as you started. Take a few steps, then ask for a few more steps in the haunches-in again.

This will be the first time you ask the horse to bend in the direction he is moving, as opposed to the leg-yield or shoulder-in, where he is flexed or bent away from the direction in which he is moving. Practice shoulder-in to haunches-in (diagram page 48).

Here I am with Felix at the angle judges want to see a horse doing the travers, or haunches-in, on three tracks.

Sometimes this four-track approach is used in schooling, but it's too much angle for the show arena.

HAUNCHES-OUT

When you feel confident with haunches-in, it's time to try renvers (pronounced rahn-vayr), the haunches-out. Just think of it as a shoulder-in with the bend in the opposite direction. Your building blocks will help you here, since the horse knows both shoulder-in and travers. This is just a different angle.

Coming out of the corner, position your horse's shoulders slightly to the inside, at the same angle as if you were riding shoulder-in. Then straighten and change the bend, asking the horse to curve around your opposite leg, which should now be at the girth, while your new outside leg is behind the girth. The haunches-out leg position is the opposite of the shoulder-in leg position.

Perform all these movements (leg-yield, shoulder-in, haunches-in, haunches-out) at both the walk and trot, and you'll have dealt with the trot work required through Second Level. See, it wasn't hard, was it? This should give you a very solid foundation for the basics you will build on at Third Level and above. Do not, however, underestimate the time you must take to practice and perfect each and every one of these movements. Expect to make them part of your daily training forever.

Felix is schooling renvers (haunches-out). Notice the shoulders are off the track, rather than the hocks being thrown to the outside. This horse is showing the proper amount of bend for Second Level. More bend in the neck would be incorrect.

Quality of the Gaits

Quality of the gaits is a vital consideration and one that should be kept at the forefront as you do your work. You are trying to develop a horse who is naturally relaxed in his back, moving freely forward in the contact and who, when asked, will stretch long and low. Flashy movement does not equal quality of the gaits, so don't push for it if everything else is not in place. It comes with time from a horse thoroughly enjoying his work, who is relaxed and supple—that is, showing freedom of movement—in the connection. Expression, or if you want to use a trendy term, "bling," can be manufactured to some extent, but a 5-foot woman isn't going to be able to produce it if the horse isn't willing to give it. Expression only comes from a horse proud and happy in his work, and it can show itself in different ways. Keep monitoring the quality of the gait as you work. If it becomes jeopardized in a lateral movement, get out of it for a moment, get the quality back while moving straight ahead and then re-address the lateral movement. Once you train a horse to do a lateral movement incorrectly, it's 10 times harder to fix the problem than doing it correctly from the beginning.

Until your horse is stronger and more collected, it's difficult to have the angle in the half-pass as steep as a shoulder-in without losing the quality of the gait. Only increase the steepness of the angle to the degree that you're able to maintain the quality of the gait.

Shoulder-in into Haunches-in

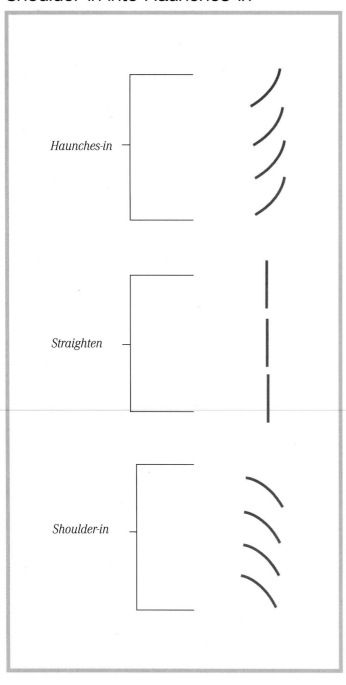

Haunches-in

Straighten

Shoulder-in

HALF-PASS

When you move up to Third Level, you'll need to do a half-pass at the trot. Once you've established the shoulder-in and haunches-in, the foundation for your trot half-pass is already built. In this movement, the horse bends in the direction he's going, with the shoulders slightly leading. The bend in the neck should never be more than enabling you to see just the corner of the eye.

If you think of nothing more than a haunches-in on a diagonal line, you will have a half-pass. As always, the degree of bend should only be as steep as the angle you're riding.

In a half-pass, you and your horse should both be looking toward the letter that is your destination. As with the leg-yield, I always want the horse to move to that destination on his own, rather than feeling as if I'm pushing him sideways. If I'm not able to accomplish this with my inside leg encouraging the horse to step forward, I will straighten him on the diagonal line I've been traveling, ride a few steps of medium trot to gain momentum and then attempt to take him back to the half-pass.

If you feel as if the horse is not listening to your outside leg, turn the half-pass into a leg-yield and for a few strides, push the horse off your outside leg to make him more sensitive to your aids. Doing this also prevents him from popping out his outside shoulder and supples him through the neck, which in turn gives you more control of the shoulder.

This exercise comes in handy when you're in the show ring and the horse starts to slow down and back off. When he feels you take a little firmer hold on the outside rein and put your outside leg on, he thinks he's going to be pushed into a leg-yield, so he starts getting more activated. Just get his attention with this tactic; don't let him go into the leg-yield when you're being judged. That should be enough to energize him in the half-pass so you can continue that movement.

This is an advanced half-pass showing a dynamic cross-over, demonstrated in the Prix St. Georges by 1996 Olympic team bronze medalist Michelle Gibson and Elite European Sport Horses' Lex Barker. Both horse and rider are looking toward their destination on their way to winning the 2006 Collecting Gaits Farm/U.S. Equestrian Federation Intermediaire I championship with a clean sweep of three competitions.

In the half-pass, it's important that you don't keep your leg or spur continually on the horse. That will only diminish the quality of your trot and make the horse dull to your aids.

Straightness

Don't start working on collection until your horse is moving straight at the walk, trot and canter. Achieving straightness is harder than it sounds, because no horse is straight by nature. All horses have a stiff side and a hollow side. Determining which side is stiff on your horse is part of getting to know him.

If, for instance, the horse is stiff to the left, then the left shoulder would be popping out; that is, he would be heavier in the left rein and want to bend too much to the right. Very crooked horses will step short on the hollow (right) side in some cases.

When trying to straighten a horse, the idea is to loosen him on the stiff side, while encouraging him to seek more contact on the hollow side. If your horse is stiff to the left, try tracking right at the trot. Stay off the rail a few meters and ride a renvers (haunches-out); this will make the horse give in his whole body to the left and soften him on the left rein. When your horse gives up the tension on the left side, you automatically will have more contact on the right rein and a softer contact on the left. You need to feel when the horse is trying to get softer on the stiff side. Let him travel straight for a few steps after the renvers to re-assess how he feels. If he hasn't softened, go into renvers again.

Another useful exercise involves the travers (haunches-in). Circle in the direction of the stiff side and, using a leg-yield, make your circle bigger, trying to get softer on the inside rein. You can also do haunches-in on the 20-meter circle and then take it back to the leg-yield on the circle again. Keep moving back and forth between the two until you feel your horse take more contact on the outside rein and get softer in the inside rein. This will free up the horse on the stiff side and make it possible to take more feel on the hollow (outside) rein. When the horse gives it up, you should feel as if the inside connection is like butter in your hand.

But don't get too obsessed with these exercises and feel like your horse has to be perfect today! Be patient; it takes time to get the horse to feel more equal in both reins and be straight in his body.

Remember that to determine whether your horse is straight, he should be on only two tracks as you look at him head-on in the mirror, and you should be riding with an even connection. It is not necessarily true that if your connection is uneven, the horse won't be straight. But in that case, you still would have problems at some point in some movement.

This is a huge flying change. Felix is very uphill and this picture shows the freedom of the horse's front end. This photo was taken when Felix had been doing one-tempis for only two months.

CHAPTER 5

Making Progress

AFTER YOU'VE PRACTICED AND PERFECTED A CLEAN WALK/CANTER TRANSITION, address the canter with a little haunches-in and shoulder-in—or rather, shoulder-fore, at slightly less of an angle than shoulder-in. Use the shoulder-fore and haunches-in to increase suppleness and strength in the hind end, in preparation for the counter-canter, canter half-passes and flying changes to come.

To get started, establish your canter, then ride shoulder-fore for a few strides, making sure the quality is still good. Next, straighten the horse and let him lengthen for a few strides, then bring him back into the shoulder-fore position. Repeat this a few times until the horse comes back easily, you're able to bring the shoulders slightly to the inside, and can lengthen again at will. You need to have that adjustability in your canter. Once you've established this and believe the horse understands the concept, do the same exercise in haunches-in, making sure you have full control of the haunches and the amount of bend.

Counter-Canter 1A

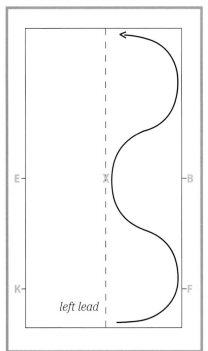

left lead

COUNTER-CANTER

Next, we'll start the counter-canter. This is another extremely good exercise for teaching a horse balance, straightness and a good connection on the outside rein.

From the center of the short side, plan to do a shallow serpentine on the long side. Cut the corner and head toward V. Don't go over the centerline so you can keep it shallow. Then let the horse go back to the rail and continue (see counter-canter diagram 1A, left).

Now we're going to concentrate on the canter:

■ **First, you must deal with the counter-canter to get the horse supple through the outside rein, a key to all our other work in this chapter.**

■ **Next, we'll tackle the canter half-pass, which really isn't intimidating when you have the trot half-pass down pat.**

■ **Then we'll master flying changes by coordinating aids and timing. If your timing is not right, you'll never get a proper change.**

■ **And finally, we're going to try the tempis, multiple changes of lead.**

Counter-Canter 1B

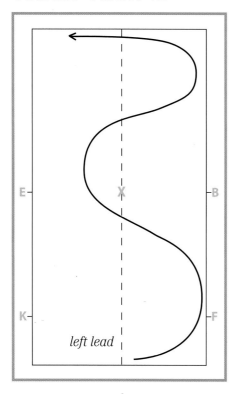

left lead

Counter-Canter 2

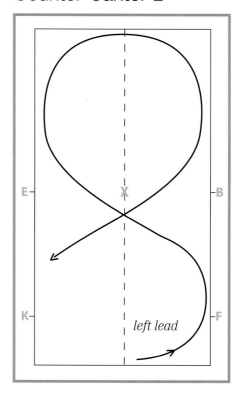

left lead

Not until you feel this is becoming easier for the horse should you make it any steeper or more difficult by increasing the amount of distance from the rail (see counter-canter diagram 1B, above).

Once you feel the horse is doing this exercise relatively easily, take him on the short diagonal and go through the short end on the counter-lead (see counter-canter diagram 2, above).

Let me walk you through it: If you're on the left

lead, canter from F to E on the diagonal, then go down the long side, cutting the corner a little bit.

Leave enough room so you can guide the horse back toward the rail if you feel he is leaning too much to the inside. Then come back from B to K onto the true lead. This lets you experience the counter-canter without keeping the horse in it for too long.

Just be careful you're not holding the horse up with the inside/lead rein. Do not overbend the horse's neck towards the lead, either. You must stay connected on the outside rein. Keep in mind as you're riding the counter-canter that your goal is to keep the horse as straight as possible.

Check your legs, making sure it's clear in the horse's mind that **your** inside leg (the one on the same side as the horse's leading leg) is slightly forward and your outside leg is slightly back. You should keep the horse slightly less bent in the counter-canter than on the true lead because it's harder for him to balance. Horses have a tendency to lean more on the outside rein in the counter-canter, so always work for a horse who feels as if he is between both reins and legs.

check box ✓

When I'm referring to inside rein and outside rein, it's in conjunction with the lead you're on. So on the right lead, your right rein is the inside rein, and when you switch to counter-canter it is still going to be your inside rein. Confusing, I know, but think of it while you're riding, and it will be easier.

Jane Thomas demonstrates at my request what happens when you try to overbend a horse to keep him on the counter-lead, rather than having him balanced between the rider's hands and legs. This photo clearly shows that the horse becomes low in the poll, short in the neck and falls onto the left shoulder. It's a real temptation to bend your horse's neck more than you should—but don't do it.

The goal here is not just the counter-canter, which is so useful for getting the horse supple through the outside rein, but also preparing him to learn flying changes after you have the simple changes of lead down pat.

CANTER HALF-PASS

Actually, a canter half-pass by itself is no more difficult than the trot half-pass; think of doing a haunches-in on a diagonal line (see canter half-pass diagram 1, page 60).

The important thing with half-pass is being able to control the shoulders. The amount of bend and collection depends on the steepness of the angle, as I've said before. Of course, as in the half-pass at the trot, the haunches should never lead the shoulders, and the horse must be looking where he's going—put the letter that is your destination between your horse's ears.

The horse doing a half-pass for Third Level or even Prix St. Georges will require less angle and thus less

Be sure that you have quality in the canter, as it will determine the quality of the change.

bend than the half-pass required in the tests at the Grand Prix level. The amount of bend and collection will increase as you go up through the levels (see canter half-pass diagram 2, page 60).

At the time I'm writing this book, at Third Level you will do a half-pass into a single flying change. At Grand Prix, you'll be asked to do a zig-zag on the pattern of three strides half-pass, flying change, to six strides half-pass to a flying change. The full sequence is 3-6,6,6,3.

Keep in mind that the most important job for you is to keep your horse happy in his work and to develop a relationship that will last!

This horse shows good expression and a very uphill tendency, while the rider is staying quiet and sitting in the middle of the saddle so as not to disrupt her mount's balance.

FLYING CHANGES

To execute a good flying change, the rider must expertly coordinate aids and timing. Let me explain the mechanics to you, using the example of a horse on the right lead: In this case, the left hind is the first leg to touch the ground. The flying change takes place during this moment, when the horse is mainly supporting himself on his right front leg. This is when the horse will do the flying change. Bearing all his weight on the right front makes it possible for him to follow through onto the left lead.

To start the flying change, very much like beginning leg-yield in the trot work, go on the diagonal line on the true lead. As you approach centerline, turn it into a little bit of a leg-yield off the new inside lead, keeping your leg back to activate the horse. If you feel he's anticipating, do a walk transition for two or three steps and proceed on the true lead. Repeat on the other side. Go on the diagonal on the true lead, turn it into counter-canter, counter-canter through the short end, activate the horse with your outside leg behind the girth and walk. Do this until it is very clear in the horse's mind that changing the bend does not mean a flying change. Changing your leg position is what will determine the flying change.

When you feel you have the horse shifting his weight from one side to the other, take the next step. Because you have done your work up to this point in the training, he is sensitive to your aids and straight in his body.

If you are on the left lead, carry the whip in your left

The canter rhythm should be the same before and after the change.
Too often, what happens is that when you ask for the change,
the horse speeds up instead of doing the change.

Flying Changes 1

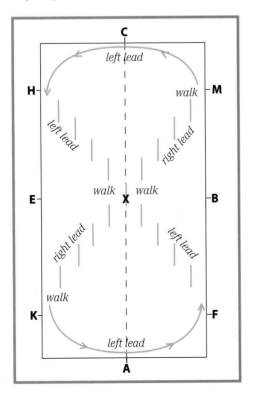

Flying Changes 2

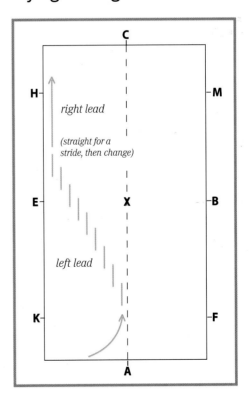

hand, with your outside (right) leg back. When you feel the horse is balanced between hands and legs and not leaning, that's the moment to ask for the change with a half-halt. Then move your left leg back and move your right leg forward as the change takes place. If the horse does not respond to your leg aids promptly, use the whip behind your left leg on your next try as you ask for the change. The timing of a flying change is what makes it successful—or not. If the timing is wrong, your change will never be clean.

If you don't have experience with flying changes, try to ride a horse who does before teaching your own horse, or you could very well wind up with late changes; that is, a horse who changes leads behind after changing in front, instead of doing both at the same time. Riders who bend their horses during changes will wind up with late changes and a lack of expression, so it's vital to think "straight."

In a change from right lead to left lead, for instance, it is important not to bend the neck to the right. What you need to think about is straightening the horse with your left rein, which keeps the shoulder from falling to the left and the haunches from moving to the right.

As you progress with flying changes, you have to tailor a system that works for you. Nobody can really tell you how to do that. It comes through experience.

I cannot stress enough how the timing of the aids is what will make the change either successful and

clean, late or croup high (as awkward as if the horse were bucking). It is also important to soften on the new inside rein as you change, so the horse can really be allowed to express himself. The job of the new outside rein is to control speed and straightness.

You often find riders futilely attempting to "help" the horse change by throwing themselves around in the saddle. In reality, such dramatic moves make flying changes much more difficult for your horse to execute, and nearly impossible for him to do the three-, two- and one-tempis. If the horse is truly on the aids, you don't have to worry about how far back you move your leg, or how strongly you use it. Just make sure your legs are not sliding all over the place. Your aids should be very quiet, as if you were whispering to your horse.

Think about driving a motorcycle with someone on the back. If she is sitting quietly, then you are able to drive straight and make turns easily. But if your passenger is throwing her weight around, it is very hard for you to keep control of the situation.

It's not any different for the horse. It's natural for a horse sometimes to anticipate a flying change as you begin work in that area, and throw one in when you haven't asked for it.

If that happens, don't get after him. He shouldn't associate the flying change with punishment. Just come back to a walk transition, making sure to keep the quality in the gait, then return to what you were doing.

To teach a horse to shift his weight at the canter, use a simple exercise involving leg-yields. Start cantering on the left lead and leg-yield to the centerline. When you reach the middle of the arena, make a transition to the walk. Take one to two walk steps, then pick up the right lead and leg-yield back to the wall. Transition to the walk at the wall and pick up the left lead. Go around the short end of the arena and leg-yield to the centerline after the corner. Transition to the walk for one or two steps, then pick up the right lead and leg-yield to the wall again (see flying changes diagram 1, page 57). Perform the exercise until you feel that the horse is anticipating having you ask for the change. You're trying to make him sensitive to the leg. That short transition to the walk gives him a moment to understand he is going to be asked for the new lead. Quickly moving him off alternate legs gets him sensitive to sideways movement. After this work, you should feel when the horse is ready to do a flying change.

At that point, come off the centerline on the left lead, leg-yielding to the left, doing a flying change as you reach the wall. But then just go straight after he changes, as a reward (see flying changes diagram 2, page 57). Make sure you pet your horse and make a big deal that he did it right. That way, when you try it from the other side, he's excited to please you again.

When the horse has learned single changes, it's time to think about whether you and he are ready for the tempis, or multiple changes. To test your readiness, ask yourself this question: When you signaled for the change, did you get it at that moment, or two strides later? Because if it was two strides later, there's no way you're ready to start counting multiple changes. For the ultimate, changing leads every stride, the "one-tempis," the horse must have adequate balance not to require rebalancing by the rider after every change. You don't have enough time to do that when you're involved with "the ones."

When the horse gets quicker off the aids, the sequence of tempis evolves, but don't try to do three flying changes in a row unless you can do two in a row perfectly.

For another test, take your horse on a straight line and go from counter-canter to true lead and back to counter-canter. Then move to a 20-meter circle to check whether he is on the aids by going from the counter-canter to the true lead and back.

Always think of the quality of the canter before the change. As you attempt four-tempis, prepare this way:

- **First Stride: Maintain quality of canter**

- **Second Stride: Maintain quality of canter**

- **Third Stride: Prepare horse for change by activating with a little pressure from both legs to get a little more jump in the stride**

- **Fourth Stride: Half-halt as you execute the flying change**

- **Repeat the sequence.**

Words of warning: When you start the tempis, don't count at first to keep track of them. And never try doing more than three changes in the beginning. Be happy with one or two at first. I often see riders thinking they must do a full line of changes right away, and then the quality goes down the tubes.

If you have mirrors in your ring, keep tabs on yourself by doing the changes towards them. This will enable you to check for straightness, which is what you want to teach from the beginning. If the horse is getting crooked, then stop the flying changes and go to work on the quality again.

When you are doing four-tempis successfully, then it is time to play with a few three-tempis. The preparation for this is going to be:

- **First Stride: Maintain quality of canter**

- **Second Stride: Prepare horse for change by activating with a little pressure from both legs to get a little more jump in the stride**

- **Third Stride: Half-halt as you execute the flying change**

- **Repeat the sequence.**

At this point, you will need to keep track of the number of times you change, so now you can start counting. Here's how I do it for the three-tempis: **One, two, three; Two, two, three; Three two three.**

For twos, the preparation is:

- **First Stride: Prepare horse for change by activating with a little pressure from both legs to get a little more jump in the stride**

check box ✓

There may come a point when you learn that your horse is not suitable for the level you want to ride. At that time, you'll have to make a decision about continuing to have fun where you are, or jeopardizing the horse's welfare by asking him to do something of which he is not physically or mentally capable. If you want to move up the levels, you have to act in the best interest of both your horse and yourself. That means buying a new horse if necessary and if you can't keep two, selling your old horse to a good home where he can start off someone else.

Trot and Canter Half-Pass 1

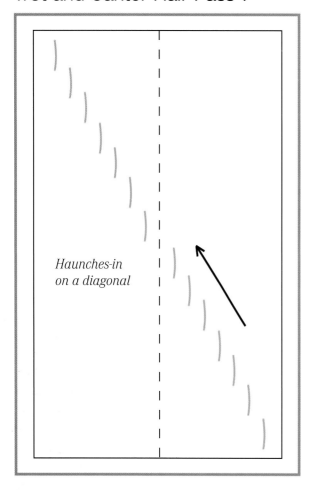

Haunches-in on a diagonal

Trot and Canter Half-Pass 2

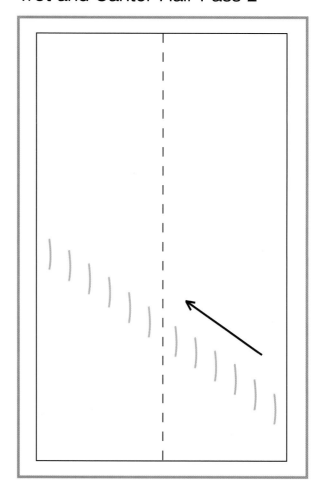

- **Second Stride: Half-halt as you execute the flying change**
- **Repeat the sequence.**

Counting for the twos works this way: **One, two; Two, two; Three, two.**

When you can do twos without a problem, then you can play with a couple of one-tempis. As I've said, the horse at this point must stay balanced on his own, because there is no time to prepare between changes.

This is a good test to see just how sensitive your horse is. I start with the true lead on a 20-meter circle, asking for only one change at first. In this situation, the horse naturally will want to come back to the true lead, which makes the change easy and sets the horse up for success. After I can do two changes in a row, I take the one-tempis to a straight line and try that. Be patient, since ones are not easy if you have never done them before. The key to success here, as I've been saying throughout the book, is a horse who is sensitive to the aids—and a rider who has a good seat and independent aids.

Remember that even though I am talking about learning to count up to ones, you should never try and teach these all at once. The most important thing is to make sure that you keep your horse happy and enjoying the work. Always reward a positive response and keep in your mind what level you are working for.

Once you have mastered flying changes, it's time to think about how they will play a role in what is required for your test. For instance, you will be doing changes from canter half-passes.

CHAPTER 6

Recipes for Dressage Basics

I CALL THESE "RECIPES" BECAUSE THE IDEA IS TO GIVE YOU THE TYPE OF STEP-BY-STEP "how-to" directions you'd find in a cookbook. I also tell you how each movement acts as a building block for others, and what you should see in the mirror as you work, as well as what *not* to do (which is often as important as what you need to do!).

THE EXERCISE: **LONG AND LOW**

- **What it does:** Gives the muscles in the horse's back and topline a chance to warm up and stretch.

- **A building block for:** Confidence and relaxation; improved connection and throughness.

- **How to do it:** Start with a good connection and push the horse gently up to the bridle. Let the horse gradually and gently take the reins and reach for the ground. To get the horse to go long and low, push him into the bit and then gradually ease off with your hands, allowing him to chew the bit and take the reins from you gently. Don't let him yank the reins. When the horse has a good connection, he should be willing to stretch when asked to do so.

- **Caution:** Never let the horse change his rhythm or pull the reins from your hands.

- **Hint:** If the horse is reluctant to stretch, do some leg-yields at the walk, bringing him back and asking him to walk on. Then try again.

- **In the mirror:** You should see that the horse's nose remains in front of the vertical, reaching out and down. There might be a few instants when the horse is behind the vertical. That would be acceptable for only a couple of seconds—otherwise the horse is not truly reaching for the bit.

- **Checklist:** Do this periodically during your ride, as well as in warm-up and cool-down.

THE EXERCISE: **TURN ON THE FOREHAND**

- **What it does:** Teaches the horse to move away from and be sensitive to the pushing aids.

- **A building block for:** Loosening the hindquarters.

- **How to do it:** Halt parallel to the rail, but far enough away from it so that you don't bump into it

Having problems getting your horse to go long and low? Can't remember what to do the first time you attempt the half-pass? Don't feel you have to go back through the text hunting for the answers. Just read the appropriate recipe for an overview of the movements we have discussed earlier in these pages. Think of it as a mini-refresher course for what you've already read.

when you turn. Flex the horse toward the rail, but keep the contact on the other rein, so the horse doesn't overbend. Put more weight on the seatbone that's closer to the rail, and use the leg on that side just behind the girth to nudge the horse, pressing to get him to step around. Your other leg should remain at the girth. When you have finished the turn, you can walk on to straighten your horse.

- **Caution:** Be careful not to overbend the horse. When putting more weight on your seatbone, make sure you do not lean or collapse to that side.

- **Hint:** Ask for a step or two at first, then build on that. Don't expect the horse to make a 180-degree turn the first time you try this.

- **In the mirror:** The horse should cross his back legs while stepping with his front legs almost on the spot. The rhythm of the walk is preserved and the front leg closest to the rail keeps stepping, almost on the spot.

- **Checklist:** Do not bend the horse's neck too much. Just ask for flexion—otherwise, the movement will become more of a leg-yield, with both front and back legs crossing.

THE EXERCISE: **HALF-HALT**

- **What it does:** Prepares a horse for the next movement (whatever that may be) and rebalances him, enabling him to carry a little more weight on the hind legs and freeing the shoulders.

- **A building block for:** It's the key to being successful in upper-level dressage. It's used in preparation for every movement during a test.

- **How to do it:** Start with a simple walk, then halt and praise the horse. Once the process for halt is clear in the horse's mind, half-halt by coming *almost* to halt. Then release and walk on, trying not to disrupt the rhythm of the gait. As you go into the half-halt, brace a little with your seat and back. Close your fingers, but make sure the horse does not feel as if he is slowing or shutting down. If that happens, move the horse on with both legs, keeping him straight until he accepts the contact and maintains the same rhythm. Keep your legs at the horse's sides, supporting (not driving, which would ask the horse to go forward). You want to create and **condense energy**, not slow the horse down. When you've got it at the walk, try it at the trot, but instead of coming almost to the halt, you would come almost to the walk. In the canter, you would come almost to the trot. Be patient. Half-halt needs to be practiced in order for a horse to truly understand what you want. And the rider needs the practice as well, because so much of riding involves timing and the use of your aids.

- **Caution:** Don't hold the mouth too long or too hard waiting for your horse to "answer." Make sure you give and relax after the half-halt so the horse can learn to rebalance on his own; otherwise he will wind up leaning on your hands.

- **Hint:** If the horse braces and leans against your hand at the moment you bring him back in the half-halt, move the bit lightly in his mouth to get a little more reaction to the hand, using even pressure on both sides. I call this "playing the bit," and it's a technique I use a lot.

  But don't confuse this with see-sawing and wagging the horse's head from side to side; it's far more subtle. Never forget that the engine (the hind end) is really what enables a horse to lighten in front.

- **In the mirror:** Watch to make sure your upper body is not too far behind the vertical. Don't apply too much lower leg, because that will drive the horse onto the forehand. Aim for an invisible aid; the more you do it, the more educated you and your horse become in this rebalancing process.

- **Checklist:** Don't hold the half-halt for an extended period of time; reapply as needed, but it should be a give-and-take, not a one-way conversation, as the horse learns to carry himself. Make sure the shoulders lighten as the horse takes more weight on his haunches—then you'll know you are doing it correctly.

THE EXERCISE: **LEG-YIELD**

■ **What it does:** Teaches the horse to move laterally (sideways) and also to be more supple throughout his body, and yield from the inside leg to the outside rein—which improves the connection.

■ **A building block for:** Other lateral movements.

■ **How to do it:** Start from the walk. Turn from the short side of the arena across the diagonal. When you reach the centerline, ask your horse for flexion away from the line of travel, then ask for leg-yield with your leg barely behind the girth. Moving your leg farther back to get more reaction from the horse throws him off balance. If the horse doesn't understand the leg, use the whip lightly just behind your leg so the horse associates that with your leg to make him more sensitive to the aid. Keep your inside leg (the leg on the same side as the flexion) at the girth; use the inside (flexing) rein to supple the horse. It's important to make sure your horse's shoulders stay on the line of travel, that you look in the direction you're going and don't collapse your upper body.

■ **Caution:** Haunches should never reach the rail before the shoulder.

Don't confuse flexion (in the poll of the horse) with neck-bend. The ears should always stay level; you should only flex the horse enough so you see just the corner of the eye and nostril toward the leg you're yielding from. When there's too much bend in the neck, the rider loses the shoulders. Then the horse is not moving from the leg; rather, the rider wrongly is trying to push the horse over with the inside rein.

■ **Hint:** When your horse knows how to leg yield, the flexion is toward the leg you're yielding from (away from the direction you're going).

■ **In the mirror:** The horse should be crossing the inside front and hind in front of the outside front and hind.

■ **Checklist:** Give the horse a moment of release by moving your inside rein forward to ensure that he is moving away from your leg, carrying himself and not bracing on your rein to move sideways. Rhythm and balance should not change when you give him this momentary test.

If the horse doesn't understand the leg, use the whip lightly just behind your leg so the horse associates that with your leg to make him more sensitive to the aid.

THE EXERCISE: **SHOULDER-IN**

■ **What it does:** A tool for controlling the horse's shoulders. It is the horse's introduction to collection.

■ **A building block for:** Half-pass, straightness and collection.

■ **How to do it:** Start at the walk along the wall of the arena, with your inside leg at the girth, your outside leg just behind the girth. The outside leg ensures the horse doesn't throw his haunches to the outside; the inside leg maintains the forward motion and the horse's bend, which should be even from head to tail as the horse steps along on three tracks. The inside rein helps guide the horse's shoulders off the rail and gives the necessary flexion and bend; the outside rein steadies him.

■ **Caution:** Don't cross either hand over the neck. When you start out, don't expect the horse to hold the angle for more than a few steps. Straighten, take a few walk steps, then start the shoulder-in again.

■ **Hint:** Be sure the outside rein doesn't slip through your fingers or you no longer will be controlling the shoulders and the horse will go off the track.

■ **In the mirror:** The horse should be on three tracks, meaning the outside front leg is on the same track as the inside hind leg.

■ **Checklist:** Make sure the horse is on the outside rein. Give him a moment of release by moving your inside rein forward to ensure you are able to hold the shoulders off the rail with your leg and seat instead of your inside rein.

THE EXERCISE: **REIN-BACK (BACKING UP)**

■ **What it does:** Shows submission. Engages hind-quarters.

■ **A building block for:** Signifies that a horse is relaxed and confident in the rider and demonstrates that the horse is on the aids.

■ **How to do it:** Start from the ground. Stand facing your horse, take one rein in either hand, apply a little pressure to the mouth and ask him to back up, saying "Back." The minute one step is taken backward, release the pressure and praise him. When that's established from the ground, try it from the saddle with equal pressure on the reins. Sit light, move both of your legs back **slightly** and the moment a backward step is taken, release and praise him.

■ **Caution:** Make sure the horse is comfortable backing up before you start addressing crookedness. Do not let him go behind the vertical or run backwards.

■ **Hint:** When you're trying to get the rein-back straight, instead of moving the haunches over to be in line with the shoulders, move the shoulders over to be in line with the haunches. Make sure you sit a little lighter in the saddle (keep your weight **slightly** forward off your seat).

■ **In the mirror:** Your horse should be lifting his front legs and placing them down. If he drags his front legs and falls behind the vertical, ask him to walk forward and try again. He should move his legs diagonally in a steady two-beat rhythm.

■ **Checklist:** Try to stay in the middle of the saddle and move both of your legs slightly back.

When you're trying to get the rein-back straight, instead of moving the haunches over to be in line with the shoulders, move the shoulders over to be in line with the haunches.

THE EXERCISE: **HAUNCHES-IN (TRAVERS)**

■ **What it does:** Teaches the horse bend and suppleness.

■ **A building block for:** Half-pass.

■ **How to do it:** Start at the walk along the wall of the arena. Bring your outside leg behind the girth, asking the horse to bring his haunches off the wall while maintaining your inside leg at the girth. Your inside hand maintains the flexion, your outside hand controls the shoulder. Wait to add more bend to the movement until you feel the horse giving you a little angle as he moves off the wall. When the horse understands the movement clearly, you should be able to start haunches-in from a small circle—called a volte (pronounced "vol-tay")—and maintain the bend you have from the circle down the long side.

■ **Caution:** Be sure to keep your bend; don't make an angle so steep that you wind up with a leg-yield.

■ **Hint:** To get better control of his haunches, make sure the horse is bending sufficiently around your inside leg before starting the movement.

■ **In the mirror:** The horse should be on three to four tracks, depending on the degree of collection you're asking. Never expect more than three tracks of a young horse. In the show ring, that is all the judge will require. In schooling an older to upper-level horse, you may have them on four tracks if you seek a greater degree of bend, collection and suppleness. Make sure the horse's ears are level, which indicate his head isn't tilting.

■ **Checklist:** The horse's front end should be facing the direction he's going, rather than the wall.

THE EXERCISE: **HAUNCHES-OUT (RENVERS)**

- **What it does:** Encourages the horse to carry his weight evenly, rather than falling through the outside shoulder; improves suppleness and straightness.

- **A building block for:** Control of the shoulders.

- **How to do it:** This movement has the same angle as shoulder-in, but the bend is in the opposite direction. This time, though, start on the quarterline or a few meters off the wall, because you don't want the horse to feel trapped. Bring the shoulders off the track as if you were starting a shoulder-in, with your inside leg at the girth and your outside leg behind the girth. Then half-halt (making sure not to disturb the horse's rhythm so the quality of the trot doesn't disintegrate), straighten the horse on three tracks, half-halt again and change the bend.

- **Caution:** Don't overbend the horse in the haunches-out; make sure he's looking down the rail in the direction of travel.

- **Hint:** You need complete control of the shoulders in the corner prior to haunches-out. Then do a half-halt and ask for the movement by moving your outside leg forward to begin the bend toward the track.

- **In the mirror:** The horse should be on three to four tracks, depending on the degree of collection you're asking. A younger horse will do three tracks; a more advanced horse will do four tracks because you would be demanding more collection and bend. Make sure the horse's ears are at the same height, which would indicate the horse's head isn't tilting.

- **Checklist:** The horse's front end should be facing the direction he's going.

THE EXERCISE: **TURN ON THE HAUNCHES**

- **What it does:** Confirms the horse's response to the rider's aids and demonstrates that the rider has a good connection from back to front. Shifts weight to the hindquarters.

- **A building block for:** The pirouette.

- **How to do it:** Start with a shoulder-in at the walk. Half-halt on the outside rein, maintaining a slight bend. Close your outside leg and look across the arena. Sit a little to the inside, but don't throw your weight. Guide the shoulders with a slight opening of the inside rein, while keeping the outside rein close to the neck, teaching the horse to swing his shoulders around the haunches. The rider's inside leg is active at the girth, making sure the horse is stepping "through," as the outside leg keeps the haunches from falling out. Once you have a reliable quarter-turn, remember that doing the whole half-turn on the haunches is a continual process of half-halting and softening to allow the outside shoulder to swing across.

- **Caution:** Do just quarter-turn increments, and then walk forward, until you are sure you are keeping the connection and the rhythm while the horse is always stepping forward to the contact. Don't half-halt so strongly that the horse steps backward or stops. And remember, this isn't a reining roll-back; the hind legs should always be marching, never stationary.

- **Hint:** Use your whip lightly on the outside shoulder if necessary to encourage the horse to move the shoulders freely around the haunches.

- **In the mirror:** The horse should be bent around the inside leg with the front legs crossing. Maintain the rhythm and energy of walk.

- **Checklist:** You should feel at any time during the turn on the haunches that you could walk forward onto a straight line by simply closing your inside leg and asking the horse to move ahead.

THE EXERCISE: **HALF-PASS**

- **What it does:** Encourages and improves engagement, collection and suppleness.

- **How to do it:** Take the horse into haunches-in along a diagonal line—which is, in effect, a half-pass. As the horse progresses, the degree of collection and bend determines how steep the half-pass will be.

- **Caution:** Don't ever let the haunches lead. Make sure your horse is leading with the shoulders.

- **Hint:** Check the horse's sensitivity to your aids and make sure he is in front of your leg before attempting the half-pass. This will prevent stiffness and lack of quality in the movement from loss of forward momentum.

- **In the mirror:** The horse should be looking at his final destination in the arena throughout the movement.

- **Checklist:** Make sure his head isn't tilted and that the quality of the gait does not diminish as he goes sideways. Remember, the bend should be through the horse's whole body, not just the neck.

When your horse has learned the movements to this point, he is ready for more advanced work.

I do a lot of clinics all over the country. Maybe I'll meet you at one of them and we can discuss how you're doing with some of the things I've told you about in this book.

CHAPTER 7

I'm Moving On Up

BEAURIVAGE WAS THE FIRST HORSE THE THOMASES bought me at the Hanoverian auction in Verden, Germany. He was five and had been turned down at the first two auctions to which he was presented because he wasn't in condition. A man recognized, however, that Beauri had an amazing willingness to please, even though he wasn't the most talented horse, so he bought him from the owner who had tried to get him in the auction originally.

This fellow took a year to fatten up Beauri and put a little training into him. He finally made it to the auction in 1989, which is when we went there to try to find something for me to ride.

I'd been with the Thomases to previous auctions, so I knew they were willing to spend quite a bit of money, but I didn't want that pressure.

Beaurivage was the first horse I took to Grand Prix.

Bob was looking for a horse with a good attitude who would be forgiving while I was figuring out my new sport, dressage. Buying a schoolmaster was not in our plans since I had worked with young horses my whole life.

We watched several Germans ride Beauri at the auction. One man beat the living daylights out of him, trying to see if he would piaffe, but Beauri never got nasty, even though he had a right to after the way this awful person treated him. Beauri had the most amazing eye for a horse, a doe eye, and there was not one unkind bone in his body. You could see that in his expression, and the way he reacted to the jerk who was hitting him.

When I finally had the chance to sit on Beauri, I knew he was the horse who would be forgiving and teach me a lot, so we brought him home with us. We came to call him "Mr. River Grove," after the farm, because he was the one who started our whole international adventure.

A couple of years after I began riding dressage, I needed to find another trainer. It was getting to be too difficult for Hilda Gurney to keep helping me. Her business in California was so big, and getting to Idaho is no easy task. So I started working with Steffen Peters. Bob and I watched a lot of the riders at the horse shows and we decided his approach was going to fit our style. In choosing a trainer, I wanted to make sure I went with someone who wasn't too tall, because people with a lot of height have such a different leverage and strength factor than someone who is petite, like I am.

Steffen helped me develop my own style of riding dressage. I don't think I make a strong impression in the saddle. Someone too strong in the saddle can unsettle a horse. I make my body, not my legs, the core strength and try to keep my hands in a low place. I don't let my hands go up and get into the horse's face. I park my seat as deep as I can and keep myself on the vertical, not behind the vertical, which can make a strong horse stronger. A rider should be in the middle of her horse, whatever sport she's doing; otherwise, she gets in the way.

Even as my ability for doing dressage grew under Steffen's guidance, nobody had great expectations for Beaurivage. I don't think anyone ever thought he'd become a Grand Prix horse, but he did it.

One of the most exciting memories I have is beginning to think after I'd worked with Beauri for awhile that perhaps I could start to "be somebody" in dressage. It happened when Steffen said to me while I was riding Grand Prix with Beauri, "You really should try out for Gladstone this year."

"Me?" I asked incredulously. "You're kidding."

It was quite a moment, to think that anyone was suggesting I should be part of the scene at Gladstone. What Steffen was referring to, of course, was the U.S. Equestrian Team's Gladstone, New Jersey, training center. So many famous horses and riders had trained and competed there; it was quite something to get my mind around the idea that I, too, could ride at this facility that was nothing short of hallowed.

When I started dressage, we never thought about going to the Olympics, or even going to Gladstone, for that matter. It was just a way to make a living and stay with horses, since I was no longer jumping.

Originally, I thought we'd train dressage horses and sell them, the way we had with the hunters. We figured there would be a good market for Second-Level horses who had been brought along properly. What I did with them wasn't too much different from what we had done on the flat with our hunters, who had handled shoulder-in, haunches-in (travers) and haunches-out (renvers) while we were schooling. So the movements were no problem for me as I got started; the thing that was hard was learning to sit the darn trot!

Peggy and Parry Thomas love to watch us schooling the horses and are usually ringside at River Grove.

When we began doing some shows, we were relatively successful for newcomers in the sport. Peggy and Parry were thoroughly enjoying the fact that we were going to dressage shows. When Steffen mentioned Gladstone, it was very exciting for them to think we were going to try out for the national championships.

With the hunters, it had been all buy and sell. The Thomases never got to see a horse progress for any length of time. It was a great business: They'd get offered a profit and they'd take it. This is Bob's specialty.

As we became more involved with dressage, the Thomases developed a different way of thinking about the horses. They liked being able to keep them and go to national championships, so it turned into more of a hobby instead of being all business for them, though Bob still does investments with the hunters and jumpers.

A year after I made the switch to dressage, the Thomases' daughter, Jane, did the same, leaving the hunter/jumper world for our new discipline. Parry and Peggy come over nearly every morning when they're home at River Grove to watch Jane and me train in one of the arenas that's just a short golf-cart ride from their second home.

Before my trip to New Jersey's horse country in the Somerset Hills, I had only heard of Gladstone, I'd never seen it. So when we arrived and first glimpsed that famous, majestic stable, with its sand ring in the shade of lots of big trees, it was like my first horse-show experience. I had butterflies inside and was intimidated as heck, but it was thrilling.

I didn't know half the people riding, since they were all from the East Coast. Sue Blinks, who would eventually be my teammate at the 2002 World Equestrian Games, was there, as was Michelle Gibson, who was fifth in the 1996 Olympics. I felt out of place, because in those days, I still saw myself as a hunter/jumper rider, certainly not an elegant dressage rider.

I always felt Beauri and I were such beginners. To go to Gladstone when you were basically starting the sport was hard to believe. You kind of pinched yourself and said, "Could I really be here so soon?"

I had to take Steffen's word for it that we could handle this challenge—I didn't know about these things. Wherever I was, he was there to warm me up, unless he had a conflict. We did okay, not brilliantly, in Intermediaire I but the Gladstone trip was a turning point. After that, I started paying more attention and taking the showing a little more seriously. My competitiveness started to come out. "Maybe I can go on and do the Grand Prix at Gladstone eventually. Maybe someday I can represent the U.S.," I started to think.

I give Steffen a lot of credit for getting me to that point. He'd say, "Now you've got to go for *this*, and now you've got to go for *that*."

The national championships got me excited about seeing how far I could go with this horse, and if it was possible to do any international competitions.

"Do you think we can make the Olympics?" Parry asked Bob and me.

Bob, who is always positive and forward-thinking, replied, "Yes, I think we could. But we'd need three top horses. We can buy them young and develop them. Because the farm is a business and has to show a profit, I'll start with three. As I find a better one, the low man sells."

That was the theory behind it, so we had some depth. While I may have had doubts about how far I'd get internationally in dressage, Bob didn't. And buying a 3-year-old named Brentina in 1993 really sealed the deal.

"I knew Debbie had it and Brentina had it," Bob has always said.

On the day Brentina was purchased, he told the Thomases and me, "This will be the best horse you ever own. I've had a lot of horses in my life and I've never seen another like her, ever."

We didn't rush Brentina. In 1995, she won several regional titles at First Level, while Beauri continued at the upper levels. In 1996, he was 12th in the country for national awards in the Prix St. Georges, and we moved up to Grand Prix. We also took a team silver in the 1997 North American Dressage Championships.

As we got more serious about dressage, we realized it was time for me to go to Germany and ride, as every successful American Grand Prix dressage rider has done. That country is the center of the sport—Germany has taken team gold in dressage at every Olympic Games from 1976 to 2004 (with the exception of the boycotted 1980 Games)—and you can only get so much done on this side of the Atlantic.

We decided to go to the German training center at Warendorf and work with Klaus Balkenhol. I took Beauri and Word Perfect, who had been successful at Prix St. Georges and Intermediaire I, finishing third in that championship at Gladstone in 1997.

Klaus is a former German policeman whose Cinderella story and good old classical horsemanship took him to gold medals in the Olympics and World Championships before he retired from riding. We got involved with him long before he began coaching the U.S. team. We liked the way Klaus did things, and he fit our system.

Klaus is approachable and you can talk to him, but at that time, he didn't really speak much English—and I didn't speak German—so that was the difficult part in the beginning. Lots of people around him spoke English and would help translate, so it worked out to some extent. But I laugh now when I think about how I didn't get a lot of what he was saying. I learned mostly by watching, not only Klaus but also multi-Olympic gold medalist Nicole Uphoff and others who rode at Warendorf, which I found to be a cold and rather forbidding facility. But this stay helped me realize there was another whole level I didn't know existed.

U.S. coach Klaus Balkenhol and I have a fruitful working relationship that has continued to develop over the years.

While I was there, I lived with a family with whom I still keep in touch. None of us could speak each other's language, but we would still sit by the fire at night with our little dictionaries and a glass of wine, laughing and talking—after our fashion.

The riders, though, were not so friendly in general, and mostly ignored me. An exception was Isabell Werth, best known for her Olympic gold medals with Gigolo, who would always say hello and ask how I was doing. When Bob and I went to functions over there, however, we sometimes would sit for hours at a table with people who would speak only in German in our presence—even though they could speak perfect English when they wanted to.

On that first training trip, I stayed three months, an eternity that was tough on my marriage and under other circumstances could have led to divorce. At that point, I couldn't imagine what I might gain was worth the misery I was suffering and what I was putting my family through in my absence.

But it was something my sponsor wanted, and all of us were eager to know how far I could go. In any sport, when you are focused on going to the top, you have to make these kinds of sacrifices. The few minutes you spend in the ring or joyfully waving from the medals podium are far outnumbered by the countless hours, days, weeks and months you spend training.

And truthfully, I came home definitely more knowledgeable and with a better concept of what it was going to take to be a Grand Prix rider, as well as how much further I had to go. I went there feeling I knew quite a bit, but as it turned out, I really didn't know anything.

The few minutes you spend in the ring or joyfully waving from the medals podium are far outnumbered by the countless hours, days, weeks and months you spend training.

Because it was so hard on my family and my relationship with Bob, I had to figure out if I could train and compete internationally and still have a life left when I came home. We had to re-evaluate everything. The turning point came when our son, Ryan, was offered a hockey scholarship to Avon Old Farms, a boarding school in Connecticut. He took it because he always wanted to play hockey at a higher level. That lifted one big responsibility off our shoulders, and then we changed our business. Bob sent an assistant trainer, Teresa Engelhart, and his daughter, Kim Koch, off on their own and cut back on clients. We turned our stable mostly into a dressage barn and just kept a few investment hunter and jumper prospects. Bob limited his commitments, which included judging, so he could travel with me more often.

I still fly to Europe yearly for training and competition. If you're going to make it in dressage, you have to go over there. You're not considered a serious contender and compared with top international riders unless you're there. Judges may give you a decent score over here, but if you're in the ring with international riders over there, you'll find you're not getting the same percentage. It takes a while to earn the judges' respect.

In the fall of 1997, Beauri and I won the finals of the U.S. World Cup League at the Washington International Horse Show. That earned me a trip the following spring to Gothenburg, Sweden, for the World Cup finals, my championships debut in Europe.

It wasn't an auspicious occasion, even though I had finished third the week before at a show in Frankfurt. I had to go first in the Grand Prix. Klaus was quite sick with the flu, so basically, I was on my own. Bob stood in a corner pretending, as he said, to know what he was doing, offering a comment of a "Gut!" here and there while I warmed up.

Understandably I was rattled, and with a mistake in the test finished 15th and last in the Grand Prix, 337 points behind the winner, Sweden's Louise Nathhorst with Walk on Top, who would go on to take the title by the end of the weekend. I retreated to my hotel room, totally mortified at what had happened while I was representing my country.

Things were better in the freestyle, where I moved up to 12th with 64.94 percent, compared to 82.76 for Louise, who won that phase, too. I ended the World Cup 12th overall—at least I wasn't last, was about all I could say. But I was determined to do better, a goal fueled by the headline in a German publication that concluded I was a nobody, labeling me "an Idaho housewife."

My story shows how, if you keep at it, things can change dramatically in a short time. The next year, I was the heroine, as Brentina won double gold at the Pan American Games in Winnipeg, Canada, and prepared to move up from Intermediaire I to Grand Prix.

But that's another story, and I'll tell you all about it a little later in the book. Now it's time to get back to work.

Our son, Ryan, is an amazing hockey player.

My stepdaughter, Kim Koch, is also a horsewoman and very special to me.

SECTION 2
Let's Show

Elisabeth Austin, first winner of the Brentina Cup on Olivier, takes a victory lap—the moment every competitor dreams of.

CHAPTER 8

Showing

HOW DO I DECIDE WHEN I'M READY TO GO TO A SHOW WITH A HORSE I'VE BEEN training? If it's one of my younger horses, I make sure my horse and I are comfortable schooling a level above the level at which I'm going to show.

When your horse has all the movements down pat, as if they're second nature, he will have confidence when he goes into the arena. He won't perform his best if he's still a little unsure and not feeling 100-percent comfortable about what he has to do. Showing is stressful enough without that added edge of unfamiliarity.

When you get to Grand Prix, obviously there is no level above that, so my rule doesn't work there. In that case, the checklist for me is knowing the horse truly can perform the test at home pretty much error-free. I don't want to feel, "Oh my gosh, here comes the passage,"or, "Oh no, it's time for the one-tempis." We all know the unexpected happens at a show anyway, so you need to feel the movements are going well at home before you attempt them at a show. Pushing a horse beyond what he is ready to do—just because you want to go to a show—could mean a real setback for your training. It can erode the horse's confidence, not to mention your poise, and have harmful long-term effects.

If I think I'm ready to compete at Second Level, for instance, I'll first try practicing the hardest test at that level. Can I get through it respectably? A score of 50 percent isn't respectable. Have a knowledgeable friend or trainer evaluate you as you run through the test to see if you and your horse are ready.

When you choose your competition level, get down to the nitty gritty of the test, making sure you know all the ways to handle certain movements. Just because you can ride the movements at home doesn't mean you can put the entire test together in competition. Ride the test through a few times at home or in a lesson to find out where the holes are and how the movements blend together. That applies to the lower levels, but when you get to the upper levels, you don't want to school the test too many times because the horses do learn to anticipate.

Think about your goals. If you're seriously interested in showing, you should consider at what level you find success. "Success" doesn't necessarily mean winning the class. It means you can go in and ride a respectable test.

It's time you put to use what you've learned— we're going to a show. I'll tell you:

■ **How to prepare at home for your first competition.**

■ **How to get your horse used to the show grounds.**

■ **The way to turn out yourself and your horse for optimum impact.**

We'll also discuss:
■ **Bling in the show ring**
■ **Designing a freestyle**
■ **Coping with judging**

Before you enter the show, you'll want to join the U.S. Dressage Federation (www.usdf.org) and the national governing body, the U.S. Equestrian Federation (www.usef.org). Membership isn't required for schooling shows, but you'll have to pay a non-member fee if you enter a USEF-recognized show and don't belong. Even if you're not yet ready to show, it's helpful to be a member of both organizations, because they offer publications and services that can help you, whether you just want to know more about dressage or you're serious about showing. Dressage tests also are available online. Be sure to read the section of the USEF rulebook on dressage. It's available online as well, and gives you an idea of what the judges are looking for, as well as the pitfalls to avoid.

When you feel you are ready to compete and fill out the entry blank, I wouldn't recommend signing up for more than two tests a day. If you take the time needed for the warm-up into account, that's more than adequate work for one horse.

GETTING ACCLIMATED

Always try to get to the show grounds early to give your horse a look around, even if he has been there before. Living in Idaho, I generally have to travel long distances to shows in California or on the East Coast, so I generally like to be there two days before I compete. I plan one day

everything is so terrifying!" attitude. I get that type of horse out of his stall three times in one day and walk him around the arena in hand, if possible. I'll also ride him around the grounds, but make sure that just one of our three outings is an actual schooling session in which we are concentrating on the movements. It's important that the horses see and "live" the environment. The only way they can get over their fear of it is to be a part of it.

If you're lucky enough to have a horse like Brentina, who is accepting of any arena and not bothered by any environment, the day before you compete is plenty of time to get to the show. On that day, I'll school her once and then get her out again and walk her around the grounds a second time.

It's just nice for her to get out. Stalls at shows can be tight, so it's no fun for a horse to stand in them for 23 hours a day. I've been to some shows in Europe where the only way a horse could stand in the stall was on a diagonal. If your horse is cramped, try to get him out to stretch more than twice a day.

On the day of the show, if I have an afternoon class, I have a light school in the morning with lots of long and low to warm up the muscles. I do about 30 minutes of walking and exercise, then put the horse away. When I'm ready to compete, most of my horses need 20 minutes or, at the most, 30 minutes of warm-up. You don't want your

If you have to do extensive longeing and more than an hour of riding to even begin getting your horse listening to you, perhaps you aren't ready to show.

when my horse can rest and do a little hacking around the show grounds, and then a day to actually school in the arenas before the competition day.

It's important that your horse gets out to see the grounds and become familiar with them, so he's not looking around when you're in the arena. How long this takes depends on your horse's idiosyncrasies, so as always, it pays to know your horse well. Some horses can go to different environments and seemingly never be affected by a thing, stepping into the arena as if they have been there all their lives. Others get to a show and have an "Oh my,

horse exhausted or sour before he faces the judges. You'll need to start your preparations long before warm up, however, making sure you have plenty of time to get your horse well groomed and ready before you hop on. If the arena where I'll be competing is far from the stabling area, I give myself extra time to get to the place where I can do that 20-minute warm-up. Having to rush can leave you and your horse in a tizzy with jangled nerves. If you're panicked, you won't be able to concentrate on the task at hand—your test.

In some instances, it's better to scratch than to

push the issue. Just consider the trip to the show a scouting expedition and another step in your horse's education, rather than risking a confrontation or a disaster in the ring. Again, know your horse. Some horses may need to go to a small show or two as a tag-along, just to get used to that environment before they are asked to compete.

ZEROING IN

With all the thought you give to your horse, don't forget yourself. To get in focus for a major competition, I like to have some time alone before my ride. Everyone around me knows that an hour before the test, I get quiet and start to go into that mode. Earlier on the day of the competition, or the day before my test, I try to find a time when the arena is fairly quiet. I like to get close to the arena floor, or at least sit in the stands and think how I want the ride to go, concentrating on the positive and banishing the negative ("What if he spooks at that food truck?") from my mind.

I believe you get a better result with positive thinking. That said, you need a Plan B should things go wrong in the arena. You must be able to think quickly, forget what just happened if there's a problem, and focus on the next movement.

For instance, say I'm coming into the zig-zag (the canter half-pass in the Grand Prix) and I do the first couple of zigs pretty well. On the third one, however, I add an extra stride—or my lead change is not 100-percent clean. I have to keep counting and move on in my brain because the next movement is right on top of me. I can't think about what I've just done. I have to think about what I'm doing next. When this happens to you, don't let your test fall apart because you have had one mistake. You can get a pretty good mark if that's your only glitch, and you owe it to your horse to give him guidance so that the rest of his experience is a good one.

Bling

I think a little bling, or sparkle, is becoming more accepted in our sport these days. In good taste, it's fun and makes things a little less stuffy without being ostentatious. It works against the stereotype of the dressage rider, often thought of as being so uniform-oriented and resistant to change.

For our U.S. teams, it has become a tradition to have red, white and blue browbands for every competition, donated by a company called People on Horses. The browbands for the Olympics were not the same as the ones for the 2002 WEG, for instance. It's fun to have something to set us apart, and many riders enjoy expressing their individuality with distinctive browbands.

Brentina proudly models her bling browband from People on Horses.

I am not a fan of sparkly spurs or stirrups in a major competition, however. To my mind, those spurs and stirrups draw too much attention to areas that perhaps should not be scrutinized too closely. I feel that way particularly because of my short legs! But I can see where juniors and amateurs could have fun with them.

Although I am not ready to accept too much bling, it doesn't mean that you can't enjoy it. I am sure it is going to be more universally acknowledged in another year or two. In the meantime, if you are not sure how a judge will react, be safe by erring on the conservative side.

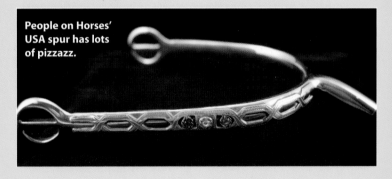

People on Horses' USA spur has lots of pizzazz.

Heather Blitz gets a last-minute polish before going into the ring on Arabella. Looking your best is a big part of the showmanship that is vital to winning.

Even when I was riding at the lower levels, I trained my brain not to dwell on the past, but rather to look toward the future. Whether you're doing a Training Level test or a Grand Prix test, there are a lot of things that will be going on in your mind, and you have to be disciplined. The ability to focus and move ahead is one of the key things that makes a really good dressage rider, as opposed to one who can't seem to get over that mistake in the beginning. If you lose focus, the snowball effect can pretty much throw off the whole test.

DRESS REHEARSAL

Before you go to a show, I suggest you hold a mock horse show at your farm, or take your horse to a friend's farm or training center nearby.

Do everything the way you would at a regular show, and get a group of people to sit around the arena and watch. You can even make the occasion into a pizza party. Warm up as you would at a real show. If there are two different arenas, use one for your warm-up and the other for your test. If there's only one ring, warm up there, then leave the arena. Wait a minute and come back in to start your test. Make yourself think it's the real show, so if you have a mistake, you have to go on. Don't say, "I'm at home, so I'm going to fix this and try again." Remember, you're trying to teach your brain to go on to the next movement.

If your mock horse show happens to be at home, try to give your horse a whole different mindset. Play music

home barn, being on your horse's own turf generally will be a disadvantage. Your horse knows what the arena looks like on a day-to-day basis, and it never changes. So if there are umbrellas shading a group of tables and 200 people at the arena with napkins flying around in the breeze, music playing and someone sitting in the judge's box or trailer, you might all of a sudden have a horse who won't go to the other end of your home arena. It can be embarrassing!

Those are situations you have to deal with, so don't panic or get too reactive in your body language, because the horse will pick up on that. The best thing to do is walk around the outside of the arena calmly, so the horse has a moment to take it all in before you start your test.

I've seen some riders who, thinking their horse might shy, come barreling into the arena as if that's going to make the horse do what they want. Actually, the horse will feel more insecure if he's handled that way.

APPEARANCE COUNTS

Just as important as how the horse goes is how you both look. Even if you're an amateur, your appearance should be polished and professional. Just because you're competing at Training Level doesn't mean you should be less pristine than the Grand Prix rider. You want to send the right message.

We already talked about hats and boots in Chapter 2, so now we'll deal with other accoutrements that you must consider.

Just as important as how the horse goes is how you both look.
Even if you're an amateur, your appearance should be polished and professional.

you don't normally play, have a horse trailer at the end of the arena for the "judges," put up bunting or decorations the horse doesn't normally see.

Some horses are wise to the fact braiding means it's showtime, and if they're not braided, it's not show-time. If your horse has showing experience, braid him so you can make his conditions and mood as similar as possible to that of a real show.

By the way, if you participate in a real show at your

At Training Level you can wear the jacket you used for adult jumpers or children's hunters without feeling too conspicuous. At the higher levels (through Fourth), your dressage coat should be dark and longer than a hunt-seat coat. Chokers for women or conservative ties for men are okay through Training Level; above that, you should wear a stock tie. The closer you can get to classical attire, the better. There is nothing more beautiful than a well-turned-out horse and rider.

A perfect braid job.

This is a nicely groomed event-horse tail. Eventers often shave the top of their horses' tails to make Thoroughbred types look more substantial when seen from behind.

Be careful with the color of the gloves you select for shows. I really love the traditional look of white, but when you're just starting out at Training Level, white gloves will draw attention to your hands if they aren't quiet.

Used properly, whips are a secondary aid to help the horse and rider along, reinforcing the leg. But riding without the whip is definitely better, unless you feel your horse might get behind your leg in the ring. Then carry the whip a few times so you can feel you have the upper hand. At some point, however, you need to ride without the whip. It's only used when the leg and seat aren't working the way they should. Don't let the whip become a crutch to make the horse go. You can use it through Grand Prix in any open show, but not in a championship or CDI competition.

Spurs are required at Prix St. Georges, Intermediaire and Grand Prix. They are part of the rider's attire. However, at lower levels, the decision to wear a spur depends on the horse and whether the rider is competent to be wearing spurs. A rider who pulls at the horse's mouth and has a leg that sticks into the horse's side shouldn't be wearing spurs. But we are going to assume that you have worked on your position, because that is the most important goal!

The type of spur to choose depends on the horse's temperament and the rider's skill, as well as the size of the horse and the length of the rider's leg. A very long leg hanging below the barrel sometimes requires a lot of movement to get a spur on the horse. If you are choosing between a light aid with a spur or a whip and kicking the horse's side constantly, choose the spur. Constant kicking defeats our purpose—creating a sensitive horse who reacts to a very light aid. A spur used lightly and correctly is far more kind than a leg without a spur constantly kicking a horse's side.

People with dull horses who ride with no spurs and no whip will find it more difficult to develop a horse who is sensitive to the aids—and it is impossible to have a good seat and a nice long leg when your leg is always trying to make the horse go forward. A rider who is very tight through the hips clamps on the horse to make him go forward, and impedes his ability to use his back properly. Instead, sit softly in the saddle, and don't get rigid through your hips. You can bump your horse with the flat of your calf to get a reaction. Sit in the middle of your horse and feel your body move with him naturally in harmony.

I think all riders should braid their horses for every level, even if they're at a schooling show. It's a courtesy to the judge and shows you're serious about what you're doing. Do *not*, however, try to see how few braids you can put in your horse's mane. If you have a horse with a short neck, more braids make the neck appear longer. No one turns out a horse better than the hunter people, so take a look at what they do.

If you want to wrap the braids with white tape, make sure the braids don't stick up. I never liked white tape around braids, and it is not being used much anymore. I will concede that if you do a really great braid job, white tape can look spectacular, but not too many folks can produce that effect.

Few people are shaving or drastically pulling the tops of their horses' tails these days. What you do with a tail depends a lot on the way it grows, but you can pull or shave a little bit of it to define where the tail goes out of the butt. As far as length goes, the tail should reach halfway between the horse's fetlocks and hocks when the horse is working. For the best dressage look, it should be cut straight across.

Should you want a glamorous touch, you can rub baby oil around your horse's eyes and nostrils to achieve a gleaming effect. Stay away from sten-

ciling patterns on the rump, which distracts from the whole picture.

TIME FOR THE TEST

The whistle has sounded or the bell has rung; be sure to stay alert for it. When you hear it, don't panic, but don't dawdle; you only have 45 seconds to enter the arena. Practice at home so you have a concept of how long 45 seconds is, and get an idea how long it takes you to get around the outside of the arena.

If there's a place where the horse is tentative, perhaps down by the judge, turn and go past it again to make sure your horse gets a chance to see it from different views. As you enter, "heads-up" on the centerline in case the horse wants to jump away from something that he's

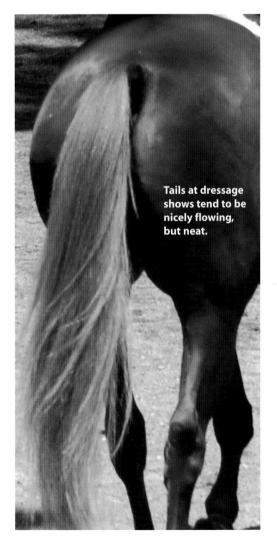

Tails at dressage shows tend to be nicely flowing, but neat.

afraid of. Should you know in advance whether the judge is going to be in a pickup truck or a horse trailer, or have an umbrella over his stand, you can practice dealing with all of those situations at home. Call the horse-show office and ask where the judges sit. Or talk to people who have been to the show and find out if there's anything that might be unsettling for your horse that you could mock up at home to prepare for the situation.

When you enter the arena and start your test, you must halt and salute. Women simply drop their right or left hand and bow their heads. Men have the option of saluting as the ladies do or they may use the traditional male salute and take off the hat, which can put them at a great disadvantage. There are some horses who won't stand long enough for a man to get his hat off and on again.

After your salute, the test

A well-executed women's salute.

riding only one horse at the show and have been doing your work at home.

If you have a bad ride, you need to be professional about it, even if you're an amateur or a junior. Don't ever take it out on your horse. If I see someone yank his horse in the mouth, I'd like to yank him right out of the saddle. That's just not acceptable. Frustration doesn't get you anywhere. Rethink the whole situation to learn where things went wrong. Perhaps your horse has a problem you didn't know about. Maybe you need to haul him to a few places away from home to work before you put him back into a show environment, or you might take him to a show but not compete.

After your final salute, you can walk out of the arena on a long rein. It's a good way for the horse to leave, because it lets him know he's finished, keeps him relaxed and rewards him for a job well done. If the conclusion of your test has been marked by great applause, it's obvious you shouldn't relax too much, because you need to keep your horse under control, although you are no longer being judged after your final salute.

It doesn't offend me if someone is enthusiastic about his horse and shows him affection on the way out of the ring. It's fun when riders demonstrate their pleasure and appreciation toward the horse with pats and hugs—especially if the ride was a milestone.

So you've lived through your first dressage competition. Now, how will you know when it's time to move up a level?

My rule of thumb is that if you're not getting in the high-60-percent range, you should never move on. I don't want to discourage you, but people don't put a high enough standard on what they're doing and are too quick to move up the levels to get to the top hat and tails, instead of perfecting their performances at the lower levels. They need to be proud of the scores they get there. To me, that should be as rewarding as wearing a tail coat.

Whether you're competing in Training Level Test 1 at a local show or the Grand Prix at Aachen, you have to do the best job you possibly can. Never be half-hearted; go in and ride your test like you mean it! If you have an error, don't take it personally and just move on to the next day. There's always tomorrow.

begins in earnest. To help yourself get off to a good start, take the first corner a little cautiously, and try to get the horse confident before you make your turn.

If you feel you can't remember your test, someone can read it to you as you ride. I won't say that's wrong, but it's always good to know the test yourself. I've seen instances in which people have gone in the ring and been read the wrong test. I don't think it's asking too much to be able to ride your test from memory if you're

THE FREESTYLE

The musical freestyle, or the kur, as it's known in Europe, is a great opportunity to have fun with your horse and make the most of his strong points before the judges.

Start by choreographing a pattern that you like, including all the movements appropriate to your level. While you have to show the required movements, you can do them in any order—and any place in the arena—that you choose.

Frankly, it's tough to perform an inspiring freestyle at the lower levels. Let's face it; you can only do so much with a shoulder-in. If you want to impress the judges with your degree of difficulty at the lower levels, placement can be a big help. For instance, take that shoulder-in off the rail and do it somewhere that's a little more difficult, say the quarterline or centerline.

Always try to maximize your strengths and minimize your weaknesses. If your horse doesn't have the best pirouettes, for instance, don't do them directly in front of the judge. But, if your piaffe is good, you want to get that in the judge's face. You must remember that your difficulty factor is a key part of your score, however, and it will go down if, for instance, you do a single pirouette instead of a double in the Grand Prix. Before making your freestyle more difficult, you have to weigh the possible positive effect on your score with your horse's ability to perform; it's a balancing act.

At any level, be wary of too much zig-zagging and turning. It's confusing. The best freestyles just flow and generally are symmetrical. If you do a movement on one side of the arena, try to do the same thing on the other side.

Once you have done the choreography, you need to find music that's appropriate. People tend to relate to tunes that are familiar to them, rather than something that's unknown or, frankly, strange. If the audience (and the judges) walk away humming the music, you have probably created a freestyle they will remember.

Even more important than pleasing the judges and the audience is making sure you enjoy the music, because the freestyle is about who you are, and it needs to represent something you enjoy.

Be careful with the music you use at the lower levels. Should the music be too dramatic or powerful for what you're doing, you'll find the movements don't fit it well, and you'll lose points with the judges. Besides, you'll look silly doing that shoulder-in to a full orchestration of the 1812 Overture. And if the music is too fast for the way your horse moves, you'll find yourself always rushing to catch up with it, which can only lead to trouble in your performance.

Rather than using only one piece of music, it has

Chris Hickey does a textbook salute, looking cool and confident.

become popular to meld several, so there is a change of pace in your freestyle, rather than risking monotony. Look for variety in volume, too. Think of a crescendo when there's an extended trot; it accentuates the reach of the gait. For the walk, you don't want something loud and hectic. If you were to close your eyes and listen to the music, you should be able to say, "This sounds like the right accompaniment for walking," or "This rhythm would be good for two-tempis."

Vocals used to be verboten, but they're being used more often today. If you use them, be sure they're not screeching, but rather an underline, or a few bars in an appropriate spot for emphasis. Get feedback from your friends. Ask them to listen to the music to see if it works before you go to the expense of matching it to your choreography.

When you're starting out, you don't need to spend big bucks. There are many choreographers who will stay within your budget. But if money is really tight, come up with your own pattern, have a friend videotape it and pick the appropriate music yourself. If you have another friend who is good with a computer and can edit the music, she should be able to do basic blending or perhaps change the tempo, slowing it a little or speeding it up to match your horse's gaits as she watches the video. While that wouldn't be good enough if you were competing in the

Coping with the Judging

We all are going to have classes in which we are judged a little (or maybe a lot!) harshly. Sometimes, you may think you deserve a much better score than you got, but don't lose sight of the fact that there is incredible pressure on judges, even at the lower levels. Their job isn't easy.

If you think certain judges are prejudiced against you or your horse, be careful to read their comments when your test is returned to you. Maybe you'll find something you can improve as you go over their remarks.

Bear in mind that if you need experience in the ring, you might have to travel far to avoid the list of judges for whom you don't want to perform. And when it comes to a championship show, you have no options other than to withdraw or deal with the judges who are there—even if you think they don't like you.

Just remember that the most important aspects to consider when choosing your shows are the atmosphere and the footing. You need to make sure your mount has a positive experience, no matter how you're scored.

You also should evaluate just why it is that you are showing. Are you chasing points or just trying to improve your horse's performance?

Here's my feeling: I'm not doing the sport because I feel like I want to win or should win; I just love the surge of adrenaline, the harmony and partnership I have with my horses. For me, it's kind of a test to see where I am in my training with my horses and where I can improve it.

Sometimes, when you're not pressured by showing situations, you let parts of your training slide. So showing is important to me for that reason, among others.

I truly love the sport, but I can't say I haven't been extremely disappointed at times. At one point, I even thought about quitting. It would, however, have been difficult because my sponsors very much want to enjoy watching their horses compete, and they love traveling and doing the things that go along with it. I can't take that away from them. And when you come down to it, competition has done a lot for me, too.

Things like creating a new freestyle make it fun and more personal. I try to involve the audience and bring them into the picture, instead of worrying so much what the judges do with it. I just hope everyone else enjoys what we're doing. It's the journey, not necessarily just the success, that is the most meaningful part of all this.

World Cup finals, chances are you can get by with it at shows up to the regional level.

If you want something more professional, go to a music studio and work with someone who can make clean cuts in the music, or change the tempo a little to fit the footfall of your horse.

There are, of course, people who specialize in putting together freestyles. I choreograph my own and have it videotaped. I know what movements are easiest for my horse to do, and what she does best. Those are the things you want to show off in the freestyle.

Then I have Terry Gallo of "Klassic Kurs" take the video to her studio and do whatever she needs to do to make it work. We go through lots of music in the process. I give her an idea of what I like and let her choose music that has the right rhythm and tempo. Then she sends me several different pieces to choose from.

I don't ride my freestyle to music all that often, but I do listen to the music in the car. You need to know your music well enough so you can figure out where to cut a corner if you're running behind, or where you can incorporate a bit of a delay if you're running ahead of it. Be flexible enough so that you can improvise. If you're doing a line of three-tempis and miss some, maybe you can fit in another line of changes elsewhere.

While this is workable at the lower levels, when you

When I was gearing up for the 2005 World Cup finals, I decided I would make a freestyle that was entertaining, not just for me, but one the crowd could appreciate so they would know where I was coming from. I always loved Aretha Franklin and that era of music and wanted to try incorporating her song "Respect" into the freestyle. At times, I've felt Brentina hasn't been given the respect she deserves. This freestyle was my way of having fun and saying to the judges, "We *do* recognize you don't necessarily respect us, but we're still going to be here in your faces, so take a look. What you do with it is what you do with it."

When the crowd appreciates it and really joins in, you've won no matter what the judges do. One of the most incredible experiences I've ever had in the show ring was doing that freestyle at the World Cup for the first time in front of a large audience. That will be something I'll have with me forever, and nobody can take it away, no matter what happens in the future.

So those of you who are discouraged and feeling you're not being considered seriously or judged fairly need to take a hard look at why you're doing it.

If you're only in it for the ribbon, you're putting out a lot of effort for the wrong reasons. You have to appreciate what you're getting from showing and make it part of a learning experience. Take the positive and try not to dwell on the negative. Don't whine and be a bad sport. Not everyone is going to remember who won the gold medal in whatever competition in whatever year, but if you have a good performance, that is something people will carry with them forever—and you will, too!

Remember that the judges see things from a different vantage point than your trainer and friends.

Steffen Peters, the 2006 Collecting Gaits Farm/USEF National Grand Prix Dressage Champion, does a *"Yes!"* after nailing his test, a happy display of exuberance.

It doesn't offend me if someone is enthusiastic about his horse and shows him affection on the way out of the ring. It's fun for people to demonstrate that they enjoyed what they just did.

get to the upper levels, you usually don't have that luxury. Because these freestyles are so difficult and filled up with movements, if you miss a line, chances are you're just going to have to abandon that and won't be able to show it again.

My warm-up for the freestyle is not all that different from my warm-up for the Grand Prix or Special. But if I'm going to start out my performance with a double

pirouette from the first halt, for instance, I would do that in my warm-up to ensure I have the horse's full attention.

Even if you never compete in a freestyle, making up a simple one at home can be fun and help you establish pace and rhythm. At the very least, riding to a piece of favorite music may inspire you and soothe your horse when you're training.

Amy Howard rides a lower-level dressage test on Wendy Wisz's Rosenstein I. Note the short coat and snaffle bit, in contrast to the tails and full bridle used at the upper levels.

CHAPTER 9

Riding a Lower-Level Dressage Test

OME ALONG AS I TAKE A 4-YEAR-OLD INTO HIS FIRST DRESSAGE COMPETITION. We're riding First Level Test 1 from 2003.

I want to make sure this introduction to showing is a positive experience, so I'm giving him plenty of time to walk into the ring and look around as we circle the arena. The bell rings, I pick up the rising trot to make sure the horse is comfortable and then I proceed at the sitting trot, entering the arena at A.

A few feet from X, where I will salute, I'm already thinking about bringing him back a little, preparing for the halt. I make sure it's not too abrupt, so I allow one walk step into the halt. Ideally, this First Level transition should be without walk steps, but one walk step will make the transition smooth. Remember, this is a young horse and his first experience in the show ring is just another training exercise. My goal is to give him a nice introduction to competition, rather than push all his buttons in a quest for a 70-percent score. I am just focusing on getting him straight on the centerline and good in the connection, yielding to my hand for the halt transition.

After the salute, I proceed at the working trot and track left at C, making a 10-meter half-circle at E, returning to the track at H. As I approach E, I look around to my left, always focusing on my next destination, which is the centerline. Then I look at H as I head there. In the meantime, I'm trying to keep the tempo and rhythm the same while ensuring the horse is relaxed in the

Sometimes less is more when it comes to the end product.
Remember that when you're tempted to over-do.

frame. I proceed around the short end of the ring and do a mirror-image half-circle at B, returning to the track at M. At H, I lengthen the stride in the rising trot through X to F. This is not where I try to showcase my horse by getting the biggest trot out of him. What I'm looking for here is what the test requires: lengthening the stride. It's important that the horse does not learn to become quick. The foundation for the extended trot starts now. So it's crucial that the horse doesn't get

You're going to ride a lower-level dressage test with me.

You'll find out how to:

■ **Treat this as a learning experience for a young horse; you don't have to pull out all the stops.**

■ **Plan key moments of your ride by looking at a diagram of the ring.**

■ **Develop clear transitions, a key factor in competition.**

A lot of what makes or breaks the tests at the lower levels is accuracy.

Small Dressage Arena

into the habit of running away from the rider and going as fast as he can. Whenever you're tempted to over-do, remember that less is more when it comes to the end product.

At F, I sit to the trot and at A, start a three-loop serpentine that is the width of the arena, ending at C. This is a double coefficient, which means you get double the points. That's what the number 2 on the right-hand margin of the test signifies.

So this is where I have to be a smart dressage rider and really know the diagram of the three-loop serpentine. I think of the loops as half-circles connected with straight lines. It's very important that I know where each loop should lie in the arena. Look at it on a diagram and figure out exactly where you're going to go, and then look at the arena where you'll be riding (long before you begin your test) to put those loops in the correct places for this venue. Remember, in a serpentine, you never ride into the corner at the beginning or the end. They're loops, not corners!

At C, I come down to the medium walk, making the horse relaxed and comfortable. I'll do the medium walk to M, then from M to E, the free walk. When I'm in the free walk I ride as if I were on a trail walk with the horse, letting him totally relax and stretch out, yet retain a little contact so if the horse looks up, I could take care of that situation. You do have to be prepared for those things to happen.

At E, it's back to the medium walk, and I am taking care not to be adding too much lower leg at this moment, which could cause the horse to jig. The sequence of M to E in the free walk and E to F in the medium walk also has a double coefficient.

At F, I pick up the working trot and at A,

the working canter on the right lead. By having the rider approach the canter in a corner, the test is setting me up for success. I've just got to make sure I have the horse on the outside rein, that he is not too strong in the inside hand and that my aids are clear, so he doesn't pick up the incorrect lead.

At E, I circle right, 15 meters. A lot of what makes or breaks the tests at the lower levels is accuracy, so I need to know my math. My 15-meter circle is bounded by the quarterline on the opposite side of the arena; I don't go all the way to the wall. The bend should not be more than the circumference of the circle—I make sure not to overbend.

At M, I change rein across the diagonal, making the transition down into the working trot at X. A few strides before I reach X, I prepare for the working trot with a nice half-halt so the horse understands what he has to do. I make sure I'm not in a hurry.

I trot to the letter K, where I pick up the working canter on the left lead. Judges want to see it on the straight line, not in the corner, so this is a little more difficult than the first canter. It's important that before I reach the letter where I will canter, I check whether my horse is on the outside rein and soft on the inside, making sure my aids are very clear.

Next, I ride another mirror image, with a 15-meter circle at B, focusing on where I'm going and not looking down at my horse's head. As I change rein through H-X-F, I make sure I don't wait until the last moment for the transition to the working trot at X. At K through X to M, I lengthen the stride in the rising trot. Again, it's not a race. It's about showing the horse can lengthen the stride and still carry a nice cadence. At M, I go into the sitting trot to C, where I rise to the trot and circle left 20 meters, allowing the horse to stretch forward and downward. So many times in this movement, I see riders throw the reins away and consequently, the horse throws his head toward the ground, perhaps jerking the rider out of the saddle in the process. The judges want to see the horse nicely and politely stretching out and down toward the ground, following the rein.

This is another double co-efficient for my score. I think about my rhythm and don't allow the horse to race

First Level Test 1

1	A	Enter working trot
	X	Halt, Salute
		Proceed working trot
2	C	Track left
	E–X	Half circle 10m returning to the track at H
3	B–X	Half circle 10m returning to the track at M
4	HXF	Lengthen stride in trot rising
	F	Working trot sitting
5	A–C	3 loop serpentine width of arena
6	C	Medium walk
	C–M	Medium walk
7	M–E	Free walk
	E–F	Medium walk
8	F	Working trot
	A	Working canter right lead
9	E	Circle right 15m
10	MXK	Change rein
	X	Working trot
11	K	Working canter left lead
12	B	Circle left 15m
13	HXF	Change rein
	X	Working trot
14	KXM	Lengthen stride in trot rising
	M	Working trot sitting
15	C	Circle left 20m rising trot, allowing the horse to stretch forward and downward
	Before C	Shorten the reins
	C	Working trot sitting
16	E	Turn left
	X	Turn left
	G	Halt, Salute

off. I am showing that my horse is willing to stretch over his back. When I practice this at home, I prepare to stretch the horse by playing the bit a little in his mouth before I start the rising trot. Then he will start to follow the bit down. With repetition, this becomes a habit, which is what makes the horse's brain work. Stretching down is the natural reaction for a horse when he knows he's done a good job in his work.

Transitions

What makes a dressage test either beautiful to watch or painful? You guessed it: Transitions. A good transition is like being able to stretch a rubber band and have it come back gently, rather than snapping you on the wrist. It's a lengthening and shortening of a horse, just like an accordion, without ever losing rhythm and cadence.

So how do you get this perfect equilibrium, the smooth downshift instead of the student driver jerking along as he alternately steps on the clutch and the gas in desperation?

One thing that will really help is teaching the horse to shorten or lengthen steps in the trot or canter. This also teaches the horse to carry himself. Don't ask for too much at first. Just get two or three short steps in either gait before letting him step out again. That gets him comfortable in making tempo changes. As he gains strength over the course of your work and training, you can increase the number of collected strides, and make the contrast between long and short more dramatic.

Once the horse has learned how to lengthen and shorten, then alternate gaits. Go from the walk to the trot, the trot to the walk, the trot to the canter, the walk to the canter and so on.

When doing transitions, don't allow the horse to run too far forward in the upward transition. If you feel he's rushing, immediately bring him back until he accepts the aid for the upward transition. He must stay underneath your seat and wait for the actual aid to be given, rather than anticipating it. After all, who's supposed to be in charge here? And don't let him lose tempo, either.

If a horse is not sensitive to the aids for the upward transition, he will tend to run into it, instead of gracefully shifting upwards to the next gear. If you're asking more and more strongly and the horse runs instead of doing what you ask, you have to bring him back. Make your horse more aware of your leg, perhaps with a tap of the whip if necessary, and try again. Keep doing it until you are successful with the lightest of aids in the upward transition.

When you ask the horse to come back from the canter to the walk, don't go directly from a working canter to the walk at first, because the horse will fall on the forehand. It's that whole building block thing again.

Begin your downward transitions from the canter to walk through the trot, not asking for the walk until the horse is under control in the trot. Don't be in a hurry. There are times when a firm half-halt is necessary if the horse absolutely is not listening to your downward transition.

What do you do if the horse just won't respond correctly? Play the bit, moving it gently from side to side in the mouth to create greater sensitivity and awareness of your wishes. Think of it as a mini wake-up call—"Hello, is anybody home? Hey, pay attention to what I'm telling you to do."

When you progress to canter/walk transitions, collect the canter for a few strides, using half-halts, before attempting the walk. The key to any good transition is the horse's understanding of invisible half-halts and being able to carry himself. So don't bother attempting advanced transitions—such as this one—until you have perfected your half-halts.

When you're working with the horse at home, it's vital that he learns to stand a moment after you halt, particularly when you're practicing your salute.

Just before C, I shorten my reins, proceed at the sitting trot, then turn left at E, making sure I turn *at* E, not past it or way before it. I look through these corners to where I'm going, because I have to turn left again at X, and I don't want to overshoot the centerline. I prepare a few strides before G, where I will halt and salute, making sure I don't slam on the brakes there. As we did in the beginning, I plan to take a walk stride if it helps produce a smooth halt.

An important training note: When you're working with the horse at home, it's vital that he learns to stand a moment after you halt, particularly when you're practicing your salute. Otherwise, the horse thinks that the minute you salute, he can run off or walk

*Part of doing a dressage test correctly involves your body language. If you get tense
when things don't go well, or very excited when they do, you're
going to relay that emotion to your horse.*

away. This problem can get worse as you progress through the levels. You see a lot of Grand Prix horses that don't want to stand, and they lose points as a result. Any time you halt, let the horse know it's part of the routine to stand there. Remember, he isn't setting the agenda; you are.

I always like to exit the arena by walking straight at the judge and then making a left or right turn and walking out on a loose rein. It used to be that you were judged until you left the arena. Now, the judging is over after you salute, but it's still good training for the horse to know he should learn to relax as he leaves the arena.

Part of doing a dressage test correctly involves your body language. If you get tense when things don't go

well, or very excited when they do, you're going to relay that emotion to your horse. It's fine to pat him and show pleasure in what he's done, but wait until you leave the ring to whoop and holler. And do I have to say a horse shouldn't be punished after the test if he did badly? Yanking the reins, spurring or hitting him with the whip not only makes the rider look like a bad sport, it also can lead to sanctions from the national federation and, most of all, throw a big snag into training—one that may never be fixed.

If things didn't go as you had hoped, just take it as an indication that you need to improve your horse's training, perhaps staying away from competition for a while, or dropping down a level until you correct the problems.

check box ✓

A horse must truly understand the concept of the half-halt in order to have very clear transitions.

Accuracy is important in transitions. When you make them in a competition, you should be doing the next required gait or movement by the time your leg reaches the letter where the dressage test says the change should take place.

It takes a lot of work to make your transitions fluent, so I have put together some exercises for you that should make transitions smoother and easier for both you and your horse:

Downward Transition Exercise
Canter a circle in the middle of the arena. Before reaching the centerline, ask the horse to trot. If he doesn't trot immediately, turn in the other direction, which will take him slightly off balance on the counter-lead and coax him into the trot without having him get too heavy in the hand to make the transition happen.

Upward Transition Exercise
One thing I do on a trot circle before an upward transition to make my horses more sensitive to the aids is to put them in a slight renvers (haunches-out) position, with my outside leg back just a bit to execute the movement. Bump the horse lightly with your leg, letting him know something is going to happen, then straighten him, move your new inside leg slightly forward and ask for the canter departure as your new outside leg goes back behind the girth. The horse should be ready to go because you've gotten his attention.

CHAPTER 10

The Work Pays Off

AFTER THE 1998 WORLD CUP, BRENTINA, RATHER THAN Beauri, became my focus because she was now at the upper levels of the sport.

She had been a special horse since we bought her in Germany at the Verden Hanoverian auction in 1994. We always fly over to the auction a week beforehand to watch the horses work. The environment changes daily in the arena; they're constantly adding flowers or changing decorations for the big gala weekend. It's interesting to see whether horses can handle it, or if they'll freak out and toss their riders.

Bob sits with his catalogue and I sit with mine. Both of us take notes; then we compare them and see how similar our feelings are on what we've seen. We're usually very close on the same horses, but Bob's the one who says in the end, "This one has *this* going for it, and that one has *that* going for it."

It's important, before I ever sit on the horses, to watch other people ride them. Buyers often don't realize that these professional auction riders are unbelievable. They practically can make an unbroken 3-year-old look like he's ready to go in and do a Grand Prix test. You can't imagine how skilled they are—until you climb aboard one of these horses yourself!

When we first started coming to the auction, we thought all the horses had been screened and were safe. At least, that was the case until I rode one that got his front feet in the flower boxes that were six feet high and saw someone coming at me with a whip.

I called out, "I just want off this thing—I'm not trying to train it!"

Brentina's lovely attitude, however, really caught our attention as we watched her closely that week before the auction. As a 3-year-old, the daughter of Brentano II not only came into the arena every day with an absolutely unflappable demeanor, she was the same when other riders got on her.

As we evaluated her, she had several things that worked in her favor. She was a mare, which meant she could be bred if she didn't work out as a performance horse; she wasn't very big, just

At the Pan Am Games, where Brentina became a star in international competition.

It was so nice to see supporters in the stands in Jerez.

All eyes were on me at the 2002 WEG.

the right size for me, and she was young. As a result, she wasn't tried very hard by prospective owners and didn't have a ton of pressure put on her. That can ruin a horse even before the auctioneer brings down his gavel.

The fact that she was first in the auction was good, too, because we weren't a victim of price escalation as the auction went along. People often tend to be more reserved and hold back on the first horse being auctioned. You see, they don't want to tip their hand about how much money they have to spend.

It's funny that Brentina's dam, Lieselotte by Lungau, was so unlike her. She was never broken, and she would just as soon bite and kick people as look at them. But not only did she foal Brentina, she also had Barclay II, Brentina's full brother, who made the 2004 Olympics with Sven Rothenberger of Holland riding.

On the day the auction opened, the other bidder who was interested in Brentina was stuck in traffic, so we got her for about $40,000. Although she is worth much more today, as part of the Thomas family she'll never be sold.

When I started riding Brentina at home, it amazed me that she was so smart and quick to pick up on everything. Her willingness to come to work every day just blew me away.

As people watched Brentina go up through all the levels, they were impressed. She's pretty much been a national champion at each stop along the way.

She was just coming 9 years old for the 1999 Pan American Games in Winnipeg. She easily could have moved up to Grand Prix before that, but we kept on showing Prix St. Georges/Intermediaire I so we could do the Pan Ams, which were held at that level. Until the Pan Ams, we could only hope Brentina had what it took to be a star in international competition. After the Games, we *knew* she had it.

My experience in Winnipeg was the exact opposite of my trials and tribulations at the World Cup finals the previous year. When I won the selection trials and made the team, I was ecstatic, because I was so thrilled to represent the U.S. I wanted to make it more of a positive experience than the previous time I had ridden with the flag on my saddlepad. It went so beautifully that afterwards I thought, "If I never make it to the Olympics, this will do well."

This time, I was on a horse who was favored, rather than an underdog no one had heard of. And since I had so much faith in the mare, I wasn't nearly as intimidated as I felt going into the Grand Prix at the World Cup, where I was the only person to represent the U.S. When you're on a team, you don't experience quite the same pressure as you do when you're flying solo. And in Winnipeg, we had a great squad, a bunch of women who all got along perfectly and shared many laughs. At the Games, our group of not-very-young ladies got on a bus with athletes from the other sports, who asked if we were chaperones!

I became involved in pin trading in Winnipeg. Oh, let me be honest—I was crazed by it.

All nations participating and many of the corporations sponsoring the Games had enamel pins that they handed out. They were incredibly neat, each one different, of course, and our team had bets to see which of us could get the most pins. I think Linda Alicki won that contest.

We lived in an RV village not too far from our venue, where we enjoyed the camping atmosphere but had to keep out of the way of the nasty mosquitoes. The poor horses were welted up from bites, because we weren't allowed to use fly spray. Someone thought the sprays contained illegal substances, and of course, at all these competitions, there are strict rules about what drugs and compounds can be used. Eventually, however, that restriction was waived in the name of common sense, and the horses were no longer mosquito targets.

The Pan Am Games was a great experience, and winning both the team and individual gold medals was so emotional for me. If I'm just anywhere and hear the national anthem being played, I get choked up. I'm that kind of person. At the Games, I got to hear it twice on the highest step of the podium, which was even better. I realized at that moment, "This is cool. I'd love to do this again."

After that, everything pointed toward the Olympics. There was discussion about having Brentina be a candidate for the Games in Sydney the next year, but the Thomases, Bob and I decided to wait. It was a hard decision that we all pondered at length. But it turned out to be the right one, because it gave Brentina time to become even more confirmed in the Grand Prix movements, and I was able to spend time with team coach Klaus Balkenhol, with whom I had worked for more than three years, to make sure it was done right.

Our next big test came two years after Sydney at the 2002 World Equestrian Games in Jerez, Spain. First, however, we had to get through the trials at the USET headquarters in New Jersey, and it wasn't easy. We had a lot of difficulties with the mare's reaction to Gladstone. It just isn't a place where she seems to fare very well. She broke out in welts—obviously allergic to something, but to what, we don't know—and many alcohol baths were required to bring the bumps down so she could be more comfortable and perform at her best. Of course, we couldn't give her an injection that would eliminate the bumps more easily because of the rules against using prohibited substances.

After we made the team, we had some fun times in Germany training at Klaus and Judith's place. It set the stage for a wonderful WEG, where the venue was nice and the weather was good in the heart of Andalusia.

Accompanied by our chef d'equip, Jessica Ransehousen, Sue Blinks, Lisa Wilcox, Guenter Seidel and I proudly display our silver medals at Jerez.

At first, when we heard some of the classes were going to be at night, we weren't too happy. But it was all for the best because the heat had dissipated by evening, and competition under the lights wound up being very dramatic and exciting.

Before the WEG, there was talk that the U.S. might edge the Netherlands for the silver. For as long as any of us could remember, Germany always won the dressage at these big events, with the Dutch second. Since 1992's Barcelona Olympics, the U.S. generally had been able to claim the bronze. Without Klaus,the U.S. would not have been so successful. He believed in us and made the right choices for us to get the most recognition.

We were really prepared to go one step above our usual placing. Klaus and Judith did a mock horse show at their place beforehand, bringing people in to sit in the stands, providing judges and even serving hot dogs, just the way it would be done in a stadium. Klaus and Judith always go out of their way to make us all feel prepared and welcome in their home. After all that preparation, the team felt ready to snatch the silver from the Dutch.

In the Grand Prix, I've always gone third in the order because I don't want the pressure of going last and having to make a certain score. Lisa Wilcox, who had been living in Germany for years, went last for us, because she was used to that kind of stress.

I didn't know exactly what score I had to get; I don't work that way. My idea is just always trying to be in the top three, and I definitely wanted to get over 72 percent. I attempt to make everything as consistent as possible, take a few risks where I can and hope the score ends up being what it needs to be.

I guess my extended trot was a little out of the ordinary for Brentina in the Grand Prix, because when I looked at the video afterward, everyone was saying "whoa" as we performed that movement. I never thought we were taking too much of a risk, however, and our score of 74.64 percent proved I was right to go for it.

The whole experience was great. It was something my mother was always hoping she could see. Unfortunately, she had been ill and died the year before, on that very day, and never made it to the WEG. It was also the one-year anniversary of 9/11, a very poignant time all the way around.

On the second and last day of the team competition, as it got down to the final riders from each squad, everyone was madly doing the math to see where we stood. It was truly a great moment when it all was tabulated and we knew we had gotten the silver medal, behind unbeatable Germany and ahead of the Netherlands.

We had made history, the first post-World War II U.S. dressage team to claim silver. So many emotions were wrapped up in one for me as we stood on the podium before a cheering crowd that night, the lights dancing off our glittering medals.

The final act for me at the WEG was the freestyle, where the individual medals would be decided. I had finished third in the Grand Prix and held that spot through the Grand Prix Special. The pressure was huge, because everyone thought for the first time in a long time that a U.S. rider—me!—was in contention for an individual medal.

I dedicated my freestyle to my mother, wishing she could have been there to see it, and then went into the ring for my big moment. Having ridden Brentina for so long, I know when things are going to go okay, and I had that feeling as my medley of Gershwin tunes began to play. I really enjoyed that ride. The only bobble was a late change in one of the two-tempis on a curving line, but it didn't affect the score much and the fact that the whole ride was so clean made the evening more exciting.

As I gave my final salute, I shoved my fist in the air, looked into the sky and said to myself, "Here you go, Mom. This one's for you."

I knew I couldn't have done any better than I did. What came next, how the medals would be awarded, was out of my control. All I could do was sit back and wait as the other riders took their turns and the amateur mathematicians in the U.S. ranks played with the numbers to see who

I attempt to make everything as consistent as possible, take a few risks where I can and hope the score ends up being what it needs to be.

would come out ahead after the scores from the Grand Prix, the Special and the freestyle were all added up.

At one point, they told Bob that I had the bronze.

He ran back behind the arena and told me, but added, "Don't hold me to it."

I was surprised at his news. The way I figured it, if Spanish favorite Beatriz Ferrer-Salat on Beauvalais, the winner of the Special, had any kind of a decent ride, they were going to give it to her.

That's just the way it happened. She wound up with the silver behind the new world champion, Germany's Nadine Capellman on Farbenfroh. Another German, Ulla Salzgeber on Rusty, squeaked into the bronze. When my score for the Special was announced after Ulla's, the crowd booed, thinking mine was too low. And in the end, my total fell a mere 0.075 percent short of the bronze medal.

So I was fourth. No medal, but what can you do in a situation like that? We gave it our best shot and were a little disappointed, but at least it was a great ride and the crowd was enthusiastic. It doesn't do any good to be bitter about things; you'll just make yourself that much more miserable. So I was looking ahead, ready to start focusing on the Olympics, now just two years away.

After the tension and hard work involved in the WEG, there was a letdown; there always is following a big event. I usually sleep almost non-stop for nearly two days straight after a major competition like that, because it takes so much out of me. Having a horse from whom everybody expects great things is a special kind of responsibility. We all realize nothing lasts forever, so after a big competition, you often ask yourself how much longer you can do this and be expected to be so good. Sooner or later, you know something is going to happen that will mar your performance. Every time you go into the ring, you hope it's not that moment.

The next year, 2003, I took my second shot at the World Cup finals, and this time, we hit the target—but in a roundabout way. We finished second to Ulla and Rusty, who accepted their third Cup title in a row and would go on to win the European Championship. My effort was the best Cup finish ever by an American, and I was pretty proud, especially since the location of the finals, Gothenburg, Sweden, was where I'd had my unfortunate Cup debut with Beauri five years earlier.

Here I am at a dressage show in the mid-1990s with my mom, Marianna Ryan.

But Ulla's winning smile soon faded. Rusty came up positive for a prohibited substance when he was drug tested, and a long process began that ultimately would see Ulla lose her crown, which eventually came to me.

During the summer, Brentina and I had a very special experience—and it happened at home, for a change, instead of in a foreign country.

Every year, the Sun Valley Symphony comes together just a few miles north of our home in Hailey. The 90-plus musicians from all over the country stay for two weeks and put on free concerts—except for one night that's a benefit for the symphony.

That concert is usually held in Sun Valley. But Jane Thomas thought it would be fabulous to have it at River Grove, with a freestyle performance by Brentina to live music and tables set up in the indoor arena for a black-tie dinner. It took a year to arrange, but in August 2003, it finally happened and wound up being one of the most magical moments of my riding career, especially because there was no competition pressure involved.

There was a huge orchestra playing under the stars as Brentina danced in the moonlight in our very own outdoor ring. We couldn't have written a better script for it if we tried.

We only had one live evening rehearsal with the mare, who was perfect, as usual. The next day, my number-two horse, Felix, understudied her as the video camera angles were worked out. Before the first rehearsal, the conductor came down and met Brentina. Originally, he was mortified when he heard he was going to conduct his musicians for a horse, but once he saw her and understood what we were doing, he was quite enthusiastic and gladly re-scored Brentina's Gershwin music for the orchestra.

The evening was incredibly successful. The event raised $400,000 and sold a record number of tickets—they had to turn people away!

But shortly after that, we had to make a major decision about Brentina's future. We'd known for a couple of years that one of the flaps on her windpipe was partially paralyzed, which cut off her air while she worked. The condition became worse as she got older, and the paralysis was more obvious. At Aachen that summer, it was unbearable for her to breathe in the humidity and her breathing was so rough and loud that the crowd in the stands could hear it.

Things had gotten to the point where either she had to retire or we had to do surgery. Because she was still young and in good shape, we all decided it was worth giving an operation a shot. Dr. Jim Robertson came out from Ohio State to do the surgery with our vets at Sawtooth Equine, our local clinic, just down the road in Bellevue. The same day, I had arthroscopic surgery on my knee in Las Vegas. I got home in time to see Brentina after she came out of the anesthetic. It looked as if surgery had been a success for both of us.

It was six weeks before she could go back to any kind of normal work, but then she was in the swing of things again. We were invited to Toronto's Royal Winter Fair in November with Guenter Seidel to do our first competition since the operation. It was a crucial test of Brentina's new breathing capacity, and she was great. Not only was I excited that the mare won there, but while we were in Toronto, we found out Rusty finally had been disqualified from his World Cup victory as a result of the prohibited substance found in his system. That meant Brentina was the World Cup champion.

The sad part was that Brentina never got her moment in the spotlight, so the belated victory was bittersweet. It's not a fun way to win anything, knowing that you made it to the top only because the horse in front of you tested positive. On the plus side, though, I did get the winner's prize, a Volvo XC90. And on it I put a personalized license plate that says Brntina (you can't have more than seven letters on an Idaho plate).

So at the end of 2003, we were finally on the brink of the Olympic opportunity we had dreamed about for years. And then trouble struck. But we'll talk about that after we get in a few more lessons.

> *It's not a fun way to win anything, knowing that you made it to the top only because the horse in front of you tested positive.*

Brentina was at her best in the 2003 World Cup.

Let's Ride Some More

This horse is showing good collection, carrying more weight on his hind end and enabling the rider to execute the pirouette.

CHAPTER 11

Higher Elevations: The Three P's

EVERYONE HAS A DIFFERENT OPINION ABOUT WHAT MOVEMENTS ARE MOST difficult for Grand Prix horses. My feeling is that the hardest things for them to do are pirouettes, passage and piaffe, which we have nicknamed the three P's.

What's so tough about them? Each of these movements requires extreme strength from the horse's hind end, in addition to a well-developed muscle structure that takes years to build. This is why it's important that you don't do the three P's for long periods of time, especially when you're training younger horses.

The way you create muscle is by doing the movements in lesser degrees of collection than what you would want for Grand Prix competition. As the horse progresses, the degree of collection increases. You will recognize this when it becomes easier for your horse to execute these movements. If at any time in training you feel that your horse is struggling, or requiring too much of your strength to keep him going, he is trying to tell you he is not quite ready to perform at that level yet. Or if he's an older horse, the struggle may mean he isn't feeling 100 percent. Whatever he's trying to say, make sure you listen, because you and he are partners in this enterprise.

How do you know when you and your horse are ready to attempt the three P's? We'll tell you.

PIROUETTE

If you are taking lessons and your trainer thinks the horse is ready, the pirouette is something you can start working on as early as Second Level. Just don't overdo it.

If you're not able to maintain a correct walk pirouette, a canter pirouette is not going to be any easier. So don't try it. As always, go back to basics and get them down pat before you move on. Although the walk and canter pirouettes are performed in two different gaits, they have a lot in common: bend, the connection and the circumference.

To prepare for the walk pirouette, start in the medium walk and bring the horse back

How do you know when you and your horse are ready to attempt the three P's? We'll tell you in this chapter. But first, I hope you've been following our training program to this point, because the building blocks we've been using throughout your horse's development will assure a successful transition to the higher elevations.

slightly. If you feel that the horse almost stops, then you need to bump him with your lower leg and ask him to walk on. The horse must learn that when you bring him back, this does not mean "stop." You want to make the horse so sensitive that when you take your legs away from his sides, he anticipates a bump and moves on more willingly.

I start on a circle and do haunches-in and then shoulder-in until I know the horse will stretch forward and down in the contact and not lose rhythm. When I feel that is secure, I will do just a couple of steps turning and then move out of the turn, reminding the horse to stay in front of my leg and march! The horse should be willing to keep going without constant prompting from the rider, and he should not be too strong in the hand. Therefore you won't need to use a strong leg or hand.

As you turn, keep your inside leg at the girth and your outside leg slightly back so the haunches do not fall out. Meanwhile, your inside rein guides and your inside leg bends the horse as the outside rein brings the shoulders around to keep the circumference of the circle. Then ask yourself, "Is the horse marching on his own or am I driving him constantly with my leg?" If you answered "yes" to the second part of that question, then you need to work on the walk until he goes on his own before you try a complete walk pirouette. In the following paragraphs, I am discussing the canter pirouette, but before you try these exercises at the canter, make sure you can do them at the walk.

Before you attempt pirouette at the canter, you want to abandon your safety net of the arena wall and canter along the quarterline or centerline instead. When executing a pirouette you use a more collected "pirouette canter" that is more "on the spot" than a normal collected canter.

In the pirouette canter you should feel your horse willingly and comfortably maintains his energy. If the tempo slows down and feels labored, you need to wake

Walk Pirouette

1 The rider is holding a good connection through both reins; there's no tilting. The horse is slightly bent around the rider's inside leg and it is very obvious the horse is not stepping wide behind and into the rider's outside leg; the horse should always be stepping forward, not out against the rider's leg.

2 The connection is still very good between the rider's hand and the horse's mouth, while the horse is crossing her front legs nicely. You do not see the horse stepping out against the rider's outside leg.

3 The rider has taken the walk pirouette a little bit bigger for a moment and started turning the shoulders again, so the horse is more capable of bringing her shoulders around the haunches.

4 The horse is balanced—the hind legs are nicely close together in a forward step and continuing to step around the hind legs. You can see the front leg in the preparation to take the next footfall over to the left.

5 In the completion of the walk pirouette, the rider is showing very good control of the turn. The hind legs are nicely close together and the front leg is reaching in the turn, bringing the front end around the haunches.

up your horse, get out of the pirouette canter and go back to a collected canter. Ask for more energy with your leg and then with your secondary aids, if necessary. If your half-halts have been successful in your training to this point, you shouldn't encounter problems, because you've already taught your horse that a half-halt means he needs to expend more energy and carry himself, so you don't feel as if you're holding the weight of his head in your hands.

If you've passed the tests this far, you're good to go. So take your regular collected canter onto a 10-meter cir-

the canter as you're asking for a little angle and bend. Do not hold it for more than four to five strides at a time. Straighten your horse, then do four to five strides of a shoulder-fore, which is a *slight* shoulder-in—one without too much angle. It's important the horse feels this is not difficult. It's easy if done correctly.

After you've done this in both directions, that's enough for one day. Before I attempt even so much as a quarter-pirouette, I make sure my horse is extremely comfortable with this exercise, which will take several days or weeks, depending on the horse.

*Be aware that this exercise is very tiring for the horse,
so don't do too many collected turns before taking a walk break.*

cle. Now try a few strides of the more compact pirouette canter, seeing if your horse is capable of holding it along a curved line. This should not be difficult or require you to hold him up.

Did that work? Okay. Next, displace the haunches, using a little haunches-in on the circle line, collecting

Once you have these exercises down pat, move on to collected canter down the long side of the arena, visualizing a square somewhere in the middle. Let's use the letter E on the long side of the arena as an example of where you're going to attempt your quarter-pirouette. Three to four strides before E, come to a slight shoulder-

Canter Pirouette

in position (a shoulder-fore) and collect to pirouette canter as you were doing on the circle previously. When you feel the horse take his weight on the hind legs, make a quarter turn, guiding the shoulders so you are heading to the opposite side of the arena, toward B. Then go forward again to normal collected canter. Two to three strides before B, collect the canter again and prepare for another quarter-pirouette so you wind up heading down the opposite long side. The total exercise should be five to six strides before the first turn, probably four or five normal strides across the arena, and then another five to six strides as you make the second turn.

In the turning phase of the pirouette the inside seatbone is weighted slightly. I will always use my inside leg at the girth, knowing that I can close that leg at any time if I want to exit the turn. Remember we learned to do that previously in the turn on the haunches in the walk?

You're probably wondering why we are using shoulder-fore instead of haunches-in. Here's why: 1) It's always easier for the horse to recognize where the shoulders should be going when they're already heading in that direction. 2) When you start with haunches-in, you throw the horse off-balance, making it difficult for him to bring his shoulders around in the turn.

Take care to keep your outside leg back behind the girth, so the horse does not fall out when you make these turns. As the horse progresses and becomes stronger, you can use a higher degree of collection and bend in executing the half- and full pirouettes.

I can't emphasize this enough: It's very important that the rider sit as much as possible in the middle of the horse. That is, your center of gravity should be distributed evenly as you collect the horse in preparation for the pirouette. Don't lean to one side or the other or you'll throw your horse off.

Now, you former hunter/jumper riders are going to love this: Stride-counting. A quarter-pirouette is two to

1   I like the way the horse is sitting as he starts his pirouette.

2   Amateur rider Tracy Roenick is able to be soft on the inside rein because the horse is balanced as he continues into his pirouette.

3   The horse is showing the proper bend, stepping nicely under himself. The rider is sitting in the middle of the saddle with a soft contact, which shows the horse is carrying himself.

three strides. A half-pirouette, three to four strides. Full pirouette? Six to eight strides. Any less and the horse would be spinning, showing you don't have enough control. If that's happening to you, and you're getting dizzy, school again on a larger circle. Turn for one or two

teaching my young horses at age four to come way back in the trot, so they feel comfortable when they're not moving very far forward. I don't ask for expression, but I want them to continue thinking "trot," even though they're collected. Brentina's natural aptitude was for passage,

You always want the horse to feel as if passage is a less forward-moving trot with more suspension.

strides, then go straight for one or two strides to regain control of your turning and get out of the movement. If you're doing too many strides, it means you're not guiding the shoulders enough around the haunches, or the haunches are leading, making it impossible for the shoulders to come around properly. If, at any time, you feel you have lost the quality of your canter, discontinue work with the canter pirouette.

PASSAGE

When teaching passage and piaffe, one might ask, "Which comes first?" Some people feel teaching passage is easier; others contend it's the piaffe. Take each horse as an individual and see which comes most naturally. As we all know, some horses have a natural passage in the trot. If your horse has a lot of suspension in his trot, chances are learning passage will not be difficult for him.

I can only tell you what has been successful for me and the horses that I have had the opportunity to train to this level. I lay the foundation for piaffe and passage by

because she had a lot of that in her trot. Beaurivage, on the other hand, had a knack for piaffe. When you're riding your young horses, and they start getting comfortable with extension and collection, you are building a foundation for piaffe and passage.

It's important that a horse never feels trapped, or afraid of an exaggerated change of tempo. He shouldn't worry when asked to do an extended trot, or panic if you want him to do a short trot. He must learn to be able to expand and retract. If he can't do that, it's not time to attempt the three P's. Work on extending him and bringing him back elastically and smoothly before you try the higher-level movements.

When I'm teaching a horse passage from the trot, I use my half-halts to ask him to come back and give me a moment of suspension. To half-halt, I sit a little deeper and close my thighs and knees while my hands exercise an even resistance. When done at the right moment and not held for too long, the knee and thigh can help bring the horse back in conjunction with resistance in the hand. The combination of using these aids and releasing them gives the horse the idea to elevate, instead of running forward through the hands. If it feels like the horse has lost energy, I will apply my lower legs evenly at the girth to make him more active. Using your legs at the girth and holding them there for a couple of steps will activate him and make him more sensitive, which in turn will give him more expression and elevation.

The rein contact in the passage is a little more than in the piaffe, because you have to remind the horse not to trot on. In effect, those half-halts prompt him, but you have a little more weight in your hands than in the piaffe,

check box ✓

When you're trying this at home and you feel your horse give you a moment of suspension, trot on and offer praise, making him feel good about himself. It's important that through positive reinforcement, the horse understands and enjoys this movement.

With the strength that comes from learning the three P's, horses can develop a better extended trot. This happens because the hind end is able to carry more weight and free up the front end, enabling the horse to cover more ground. But this takes some time, so be patient.

in which the horse is carrying more weight on the haunches. Horses that are too strong in the hand are generally too tense in the back. That is, the horse is holding too much tension in the muscles that run along the top of his spine, making it difficult for him to be totally through. It is very hard for a horse to develop the correct muscles when his back is as hard as a rock.

When you feel this might be happening, work on keeping these muscles more supple so they develop strength that is flexible. What should you do? Go back to more gymnastics and transitions to lay the foundation for building a stronger topline. This is critical for keeping a horse happy and healthy in his upper-level work!

Once the horse is comfortable with the suspension phase of the passage, you can take it to a little bigger passage, holding that suspension, covering more ground and bringing him back more. Just as you did changes in the length of step and tempo in your trot work, you will do the same in passage.

Changes in the length of step and tempo are the building blocks for the transitions between piaffe and passage. Just imagine your horse as an accordion.

This horse is doing a very nice passage. She is light and uphill in the frame. You can see the poll is the highest point, a clearly diagonal footfall and that the horse is not too strong in the hand.

Without a proper foundation, you cannot move up the levels successfully.

PIAFFE

There are many theories on training piaffe. Some believe a horse should be taught from the ground before a rider climbs in the saddle and gives it a try. However, I've learned through my techniques to be able to teach a horse to understand what I want while I'm on his back, and I've had great success with that. When teaching piaffe, it is important that you have a mirror (or a good eye on the ground) so you know what the hind leg is actually doing. When I'm trotting, I bring the horse way back, collect the trot and use the whip lightly on the top of the croup. As soon as I get a reaction from the horse in which the hind leg gets quicker or bouncy, I stop and reward with a pat. And if it went really well, maybe I'll even offer a cube from the handful of sugar I always keep in my breeches pocket. (Sugar is easy for the horse to eat with a bit, because it dissolves quickly. It also doesn't leave an unsightly residue.) By rewarding my horse's positive response and praising him, I find his willingness to please me is always there. This is the first building block not just for piaffe, but for every aspect of my training.

In preparation for piaffe from the collected trot, I click my tongue to give the horse a heads-up that I'm expecting a little more excitement. If I get no reaction to that, then I will use the whip lightly.

I also lighten my seat a bit and bring both legs slightly behind the girth. Some people use alternate legs in the piaffe, touching the horse first with one and then with the other. I'm not going to tell you this is right or wrong. I can only share what has worked for me. I want my horse to understand that piaffe and passage are both variations of trot, so that's why I use a light, *even* pressure. For piaffe, my legs are a little farther back than for passage.

It's very important, no matter which style you use, that you sit very quietly so as not to disturb the horse's rhythm while doing these highly difficult movements. In piaffe, I've seen people who move from side-to-side wildly, as if they were rocking their car to get it out of a snowdrift. This is distracting to the observer (sometimes I feel the judges should be giving a score to the rider for piaffe instead of the horse), and it is very disturbing for the horse because it throws him off balance. It's hard for a horse to dance if his partner, the rider, is doing gymnastics on his back. Let's face it: If your horse isn't piaffing, all the bouncing in the world on your part isn't going to impress the judges. On the other hand, if your horse *is* sensitive to the aids, you'll get the right response without acrobatics. And if your horse *isn't* sensitive to the aids, you need to go back and work on that

reaction, which is one of the first building blocks that we discussed in this book.

I try to use a very light leg, without getting my spurs involved. One thing to remember in training is that there are times when you will not be able to use the whip in competition, so it's important to get the reaction off the leg. In the beginning, you might have some resistance, in which a horse kicks out or bucks. I will never punish that in the beginning, because at least it's a "reaction," and after all, that is what I am trying to get: He's not ignoring me.

Piaffe is an exercise that requires a lot of strength and should not be done for long periods of time without walk breaks. Through trial and error, your horse will have positive moments that you need to recognize and reward, even if they are for just a few steps. You have to play with

check box ✔

I use the whip on the top of the croup instead of on the side. Why? The leg you tap will always come up higher, so your horse could become irregular in the piaffe with that approach.

it long enough to give the horse the idea of what you want, so later in the training, one or two steps might not be enough unless they're two perfect steps, of course. In that case, give your horse some sugar!

There are some horses who will learn piaffe better by doing little half-steps (very short trot steps) from the walk. With these horses, I'll half-halt, wake them up with my leg in the walk and bring them back even more with a little click of my tongue.

I will immediately reward any kind of excited step I get out of the horse and let him feel as if he's almost playing. The contact between the rider's hand and the horse's mouth in the piaffe should never be strong to the point where the horse feels he's being *held* on the spot. Several little half-halts will help the horse understand how much he can drift forward. There should always be a nice, light contact on the reins for the entire time the

To introduce piaffe, tap the horse lightly on the croup with the whip.

Although you don't expect a four- or five-year-old horse to be doing piaffe or passage, don't forget that in theory, you're always training the future Grand Prix horse.

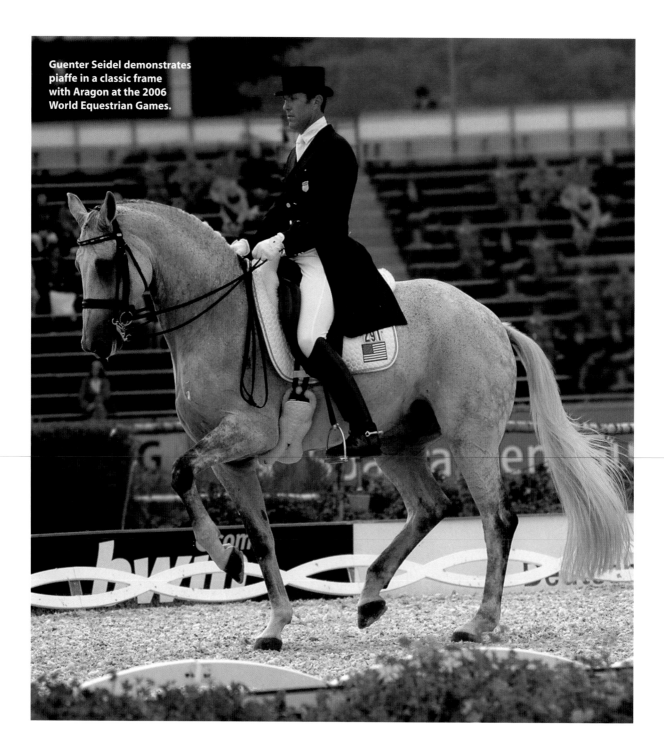

Guenter Seidel demonstrates piaffe in a classic frame with Aragon at the 2006 World Equestrian Games.

horse is in the piaffe. **Remember, he has to carry himself; you can't do it for him.**

In a correct piaffe, the horse actually lowers the haunches, with his hind legs more under the center of his body, thereby raising the forehand, freeing the front legs to have greater elevation. Of course, you know that in a correct piaffe (or passage) the diagonal pairs of legs are off the ground at the same moment.

When you watch yourself in the mirror, here is what to look for: Ideally in passage, the foreleg is lifted so that the toe comes to the middle of the cannon bone of the leg on the ground. Meanwhile the hind legs have to step toward the middle of the horse's belly. The toe of the raised hind leg only has to reach just above the fetlock of the leg that's on the ground. Got that?

In the piaffe, the hind legs are farther under the horse's belly than they are in the passage. The forelegs should be as high as they are in passage, and the hind leg, again, should ideally be raised to a point just above the opposite fetlock joint.

If possible, all of these upper-level movements should be monitored by a professional to make sure you're on the right track. Once they're taught poorly, it's almost impossible to fix. Bad habits are as hard (or maybe even harder) to break for horses as they are for people, something you undoubtedly have learned

check box ✓

Once the horse understands what you want, it's just a matter of time and strength before you start expecting the piaffe to go the way it should be in the Grand Prix—12 to 15 steps, almost on the spot. "Almost" is defined as giving the horse one meter for moving forward.

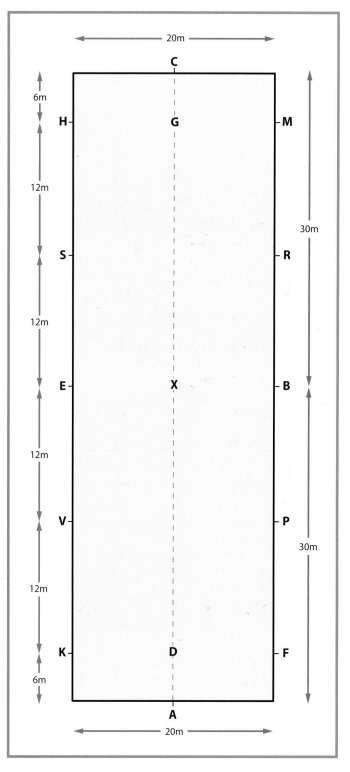

Standard Dressage Arena

Most dressage tests are held in the standard arena, which is 20 meters longer than the small arena.

Don't expect a perfect frame from the start when you begin teaching your horse piaffe. In training young or inexperienced horses like this one, sometimes you must help them find a better rhythm and balance in order to keep their backs loose. This is an appropriate time to take the horse a little lower in the neck momentarily, as you see here. Then you can allow the horse to come up in front and keep the poll at the highest point, where it is supposed to be. Ultimately, when the horse gets stronger, he will sit more and become more open in the neck, which in turn will give him even more freedom in front.

already. This chapter is meant to give you the basics of the three P's and offer you a taste of what it's about, but nothing can take the place of having a professional trainer on hand to guide you if you're serious about riding at the upper levels.

Those of us in the sport call piaffe, pirouette and passage "the tricks" because they're so much fun to do, so eye-catching, and have (classicists, please forgive me) a little bit of circus in them. Remember, though, the tricks are not difficult when the basics are there, but just tricks alone aren't going to get you a good score. So don't let accuracy and harmony fall by the wayside because you can piaffe up a storm or have a pirouette that a ballerina would envy. That won't fool the judges.

CHAPTER 12

Recipes for the Three P's

THE EXERCISE: **PIROUETTE**

- **What it does:** It is a great exercise for strengthening the hind end, but only when performed properly.

- **Caution:** Always pay attention to the quality of the canter. When a horse is truly engaged, and carrying himself, making the pirouette smaller is not a problem.

- **Hint:** School the pirouette canter on straight lines, making sure the horse is carrying more weight (engaging) on the haunches and lightening the forehand, before you attempt the turning phase of the pirouette. You should never feel as if you are physically holding the horse in the canter. You should be able to keep the horse in the most collected canter with your seat, not your arms.

> *Think "lightness" when working on the pirouette. You should be able to keep the bend and give momentarily on the inside rein, asking the horse to stretch into the contact.*

- **In the mirror:** The horse should lower his croup, sitting so that his hind legs are more under his body and your seat. That will give you the feeling that his forehand is becoming more elevated, i.e., his front end is coming up in front of you.

- **Checklist:** Make sure you are not holding the reins too strongly, which is an indication that you are not able to lighten and hold him there with your seat. Think "lightness." You should be able to keep the bend and give momentarily on the inside rein, asking the horse to stretch into the contact. Make sure your inside leg is at the girth and your outside leg is slightly back, so the horse's haunches do not fall out.

Here is a quick summary of the basics for performing the pirouette, passage and piaffe so you have an easy reference when you are learning to do these movements.

Fellow 2006 World Equestrian Games teammate Steffen Peters and Floriano execute a pirouette.

THE EXERCISE: **PASSAGE**

- ■ **What it does:** Lightens the forehand, engages the hind end and brings more suspension into the trot. It's more collected, more elevated and covers less ground than the collected trot.

- ■ **Caution:** Again, be careful not to hold the horse too strongly in your hand. The keys here are half-halts and sensitivity to the leg. A horse that is too strong in the hand is generally tense in his back. When a horse has tension in the muscles along the top of the spine, it is hard for him to be totally through. This can cause some irregular steps.

- ■ **Quick fix:** Get out of passage and work again on a good connection in the collected trot. When the horse is soft in the hand, try to bring him back to passage. I always like to make my horses think they could stretch down if I asked them to do so.

- ■ **Hint:** To start passage, begin with a collected trot, using a slight resistance in your hand to bring the horse back, while closing your knees and thighs slightly. Use the lower leg if you feel you are losing activity or impulsion. You should feel as if the horse is floating for a few steps. When that happens, stop and reward your horse to build on this positive moment!

- ■ **In the mirror:** The horse should be moving with regular steps behind, but those steps should demonstrate suspension. Each diagonal pair of legs should rise and return to the ground alternately.

- ■ **Checklist:** When bringing the horse back from the trot, it should only require a slight resistance of the hand and a soft closing of the upper leg to produce passage.

THE EXERCISE: **PIAFFE**

- ■ **What it does:** This is the highest degree of collection.

- ■ **Caution:** The rider should always give the horse the feeling that he can move forward. This way, the horse will not be as likely to panic. When it is done properly, the horse should feel as if he is enjoying himself in this movement.

- ■ **Hint:** Think of it as basically a trot on the spot!

- ■ **In the mirror:** The hind legs are more under the rider's seat than in the passage because the horse has to carry the weight on his hind legs to lighten his shoulders and trot on the spot. As in passage, the diagonal pairs of legs should rise and return to the ground alternately. The neck should be arched and the head remain on the vertical. The horse should stay light in the hand.

- ■ **Checklist:** Make sure you are not holding too strongly with your hands. Use lots of little half-halts rather than a strong, steady pull. The horse should be so sensitive to the leg that you do not need to use your hand strongly to keep the horse in piaffe.

Warming up

CHAPTER 13

Riding the Grand Prix Test

I WANT YOU TO RIDE A GRAND PRIX TEST (GRAND PRIX VERSION B) WITH ME. THE ONE I'll take you through is the test Brentina and I performed on the afternoon of April 21, 2005, in Las Vegas at the World Cup finals. There were more than 8,500 people in the stands, and I felt the sparks they were generating even as I proceeded down the tunnel ramp from the warm-up area to enter the Thomas & Mack Center.

I'd had to go second in the order, having lost my world-ranking status because I hadn't shown abroad since the Olympics. They do the draw by the order of world ranking, which really stinks. But you have to go when you go, knowing the judges won't be as generous with the first few horses as they will at the end of class, because the better horses usually compete then.

There were extra chills going through my mind and body. I was competing in an arena named after my sponsor and his late partner, Jerry Mack, so this was an extra-special moment.

And now, here we are, center stage:

I come into the arena to huge applause that matches the rhythm of my pounding heart. I can feel Brentina puff up, thinking, "Oh, they're all here for *me!*"

The bell rings, and there's not enough floor space for me to go all the way around the outside of the dressage ring, so I go right in, cantering down the centerline.

"This has got to be a good halt," I say to myself. Three strides before X, my target, I make a little resistance in my hand, close my leg to hold the mare together and ask for the halt. I hope it looks as good as it feels. I smile, salute the judges and trot off, track right. As I approach C, I'm thinking "Okay, get the engine in gear, set her up in the corner." I close my leg and go.

Once you start, you don't have time to be nervous anymore; my energy has shifted into concentration, focusing on the task I have to do. At this moment, it's the extended trot, from M through X to K. This isn't our strong suit, so I don't make the mistake of asking for more than Brentina has to give in this movement. The best I can hope for is that the judges give her a decent mark. I take a little comfort in the fact that our strong points are coming up.

Trotting through the short end, preparing for a steep half-pass from F to E, I'm thinking, "This is my least-favorite thing." It's not a movement that feels beautiful, it's so steep and

Ride a Grand Prix test, movement by movement, so you can learn how to prepare and plan for a smooth competitive effort when you're ready to try this level.

difficult. I really have to ride deep into the corner. I must get the bend, keep the haunches engaged and look to where I want to go.

As I approach E, I try to get there at least one horse length before the letter so I can change the bend and prepare her to go all the way back to the right. Again, here's the collected trot through the short end, and I'm pretty happy with how that feels. I prepare for the extended trot from H to P. I'm telling myself, "Get a little bit of engine revved in the corner and send her on." I'm closing my leg and making

Here Brentina moves out into a bold extended trot.

sure I cover as much ground as possible, still maintaining the rhythm and not letting her fall on the forehand.

From the extended trot, we go directly to passage. It's not an easy transition, but with Brentina, it's not something I worry about. I bring her back and close my legs slightly at the girth. She half-halts, coming right back into passage. Hooray, it was a pretty darn good transition, but no time to enjoy that now.

I passage to P, then continue straight to F and track right. At D, we piaffe 12 to 15 steps. Luckily for me, the passage-to-piaffe transition and vice-versa is not that difficult for Brentina; I just half-halt from the passage and the piaffe is right there.

I always try to start it as her nose reaches D in case we're a little too much forward and go past it. You're only allowed to move one meter, and although Brentina invariably stays on the spot, I can't take a chance on losing points here.

There's a smooth transition to passage after piaffe and then we track right at K. It's time for the extended walk. Going from the passage to the walk is not that difficult because it's such an animated trot, so it's not like you're moving very forward. The extended walk is on the diagonal from V to M. This is a spot where I feel the mare really shines. Once she's in the gait, she lets go of any tension and has this little sexy walk about her. I reach down and give her a quick pat, letting her know I'm proud of her work to this point.

At M, we collect the walk. One horse length ahead of the letter, I start to shorten my reins. This is a touchy thing for most Grand Prix horses, because they know the collected walk is the preamble to more passage and piaffe, and they anticipate. It's hard to keep the experienced horse relaxed here as a result.

The environment is electric at this World Cup, but Brentina handles the collected walk on the short side well, and I'm happy. I'm making sure I walk very much into the corner as I get ready for the passage. When I do

Warm-up

Here is a sample warm-up that I do with Brentina before a Grand Prix. You can tailor this type of program to whatever level you're training at, so this will give you a basic outline to adapt for your horse.

I walk on a long rein for probably 10 minutes, then pick up the reins and do a little shoulder-in and half-pass (if you're not up to doing the half-pass yet, you can adjust this warm-up to your own needs by doing a leg-yield). After that, I go to a rising trot, stretching contact down and round, doing variations within the tempo maybe 20 to 30 times during a three- to five-minute period. I'll take it forward for 10 strides or so and back for another 10. I will make several changes in direction during this period of warm-up.

Then I'll gather up my reins a bit and go to the canter from the sitting trot, bringing her back a few steps to see how I get her to react to my seat and legs, always focusing on the connection I have in my hand. If I feel there's not enough contact, I go forward and back a few times. Next is a counter-canter through the short side, going back to the true lead across the next diagonal. I'll find a place in the arena, whether on the diagonal or on a serpentine loop, and change through the trot onto the other lead and repeat the same counter-canter scenario on the other side. Before I finish my warm-up, I want to make sure I can do canter-trot, trot-canter transitions and know she's reacting off sensitive aids before I give her a two- to three-minute walk break on a loose rein so she can relax, breathe and get oxygen to her muscles. Then I start training the movements I will perform in the ring.

If your horse has attention deficit disorder, you'll have to keep a little more contact with the reins during the break because you never want him to get so distracted that you have to start at square one again. It takes a while for you to find what works for your horse in a warm-up situation. After you do, keep it the same when you're in a show environment. That makes a horse

After my warm-up ended before the Grand Prix Special at the Athens Olympics, I walked with coach Klaus Balkenhol toward the arena.

feel a little more comfortable, even when he's in a strange place with a lot of distractions.

No one can give you the right formula for warming up your horse. You have to experiment and probably will need to try it at several shows before you know what might not be enough warm-up and what might be too much. You'll need to save enough brilliance for the arena. The one thing I do differently when warming up at a show is how I handle the extended trot. I keep that movement to a minimum for everyday work, because it can be stressful on a horse. However, before a competition, I want to make sure that the horse will stay with me and is secure, because it's one of the first movements in almost every test.

Grand Prix Test B

1	A	Enter in collected canter
	X	Halt - immobility - salute
	XC	Proceed in collected trot
2	C	Track to the right
	MXK	Change rein in extended trot
	KAF	Collected trot
3	FE	Half-pass to the left
4	EM	Half-pass to the right
	MCH	Collected trot
5	HP	Extended trot
6	PFD	Passage
7	D	Piaffe 12 to 15 steps
8	D	Proceed in passage
		Transitions passage - piaffe - passage
9	DKV	Passage
10	VM	Extended walk
11	MCH	Collected walk
12	H	Proceed in passage
		Transition from collected walk to passage
13	HSI	Passage
14	I	Piaffe 12 to 15 steps
15	I	Proceed in passage
		Transitions passage - piaffe - passage
16	IRB	Passage
17	BFA	Collected canter
18	A	Down the centerline
	(Between D & G)	5 half-passes to either side of centerline with flying change of leg at each change of direction, the first half-pass to the right and the last to the right of 3 strides, the others of 6 strides
	G	Flying change of leg
	C	Track to the left
19	HXF	Change rein in extended canter
20	F	Collected canter and flying change of leg
	FAK	Collected canter
21	KXM	On the diagonal 9 flying changes of leg every second stride
	MCH	Collected canter
22	HXF	On the diagonal 15 flying changes of leg every stride
	FA	Collected canter
23	A	Down the centerline
	L	Pirouette to the right
24	X	Flying change of leg
25	I	Pirouette to the left
	C	Track to the left
26	H	Transition to collected trot
	HS	Collected trot
27	SF	Change rein in extended trot
	FA	Collected trot
28	A	Down the centerline
	DX	Passage
29	X	Piaffe 12 to 15 steps
30	X	Proceed in passage
		Transitions passage - piaffe - passage
31	XG	Passage
32	G	Halt - immobility - salute

my baby half-halts, I'm taking care to sit very quietly, keeping Mama as relaxed as possible.

As her nose passes the letter, I will start passage, since it obviously takes a moment to get into it. I like that transition; it feels good. I proceed straight to S and left onto the centerline, where we have 12 to 15 more steps of piaffe. Again, it's not a difficult transition for Brentina; she's like a Ferrari, slipping in and out of gears with those piaffe and passage transitions. I'm lucky, since a lot of people struggle with those.

We're in passage now and taking the track right at R. From passage you go into the canter. This is not an easy transition, either. A lot of times, these horses are pretty amped, so if you put your outside leg back and inside leg forward to go, some horses will take off, and if you do it at the wrong instant, you get the wrong lead. It really takes a lot of concentration and thought, so I'm intent when I turn right at R and go down the long side in a collected canter from B to F. Even before A, where I come down the centerline, I'm thinking about the canter zig-zag. You need to have your horse balanced, because one stride after you turn onto the centerline, you start the first zig of three strides. I think "One, two, then give a half-halt on the third and the fourth is the flying change." It's one-two-three change, and that's your first stride in the next half-pass, which is six strides. You have to count and have your horse very sensitive to the aids, so I'm making sure she's not leaning in the new direction before I ask for the change. We've all seen it happen where the horse is trying to half-pass on the incorrect lead. It's quite a nightmare! Then I count six, and on the seventh stride, the flying change and the new direction of the half-pass. Come on, here we go, count six again, change the bend, start the new half-pass, another six again, another change and back to centerline for three strides. No time to catch my breath, because immediately there's another flying change at G and then a short left turn and the extended canter across the diagonal, HXF.

The judges watch intently
as we execute our changes.

*I think about being on railroad tracks during
the changes to make sure I stay straight.*

This is where the horses are ready to go. They know the tests really well. Just make sure you keep them calm enough before you say, "Let's go, extended canter." You don't want them to take off. The important thing is to show that you're covering ground well and still have control, so the transition on the other side is not jerky, which could result in a lead change behind too soon or too late.

I have to do a flying change at F. Approaching the quarterline before F, I start to bring the horse back and really have her collected and still on a straight line before getting the flying change. If the change is not on the straight line, you risk having one that might not be clean. Then it's collected canter through the short end. Everything comes up so fast!

At this point, I'm thinking about keeping my horse balanced, almost waking her up a little with my lower leg, because we have nine two-tempis on the next diagonal. This is where you need to know how much ground your horse covers in the flying changes because you want

them to be symmetrical and ideally spaced in the middle of the arena. I usually count about three strides out of the corner before I start, knowing they will end about three strides before the other side. You don't want to cram in too many strides at the end; it doesn't look so good.

I'm really focusing at letter M during the changes, so as to keep everything straight and not disrupt her. I think about being on railroad tracks during the changes to make sure I stay straight.

Coming to the short end, I'm preparing for my next set of changes across the diagonal, 15 one-tempis. This is where I think a bit forward, in effect saying to Brentina, "Come on, Mama, wake up a little." Then I come back a little in the corner, getting her to set up. I wait three to four strides out of the corner, setting her up with a nice half-halt for 15 one-tempis.

You certainly don't want to lose count here, but in the Special (which thank heavens we don't have to do here at the World Cup finals), where there are only nine changes on the centerline, riders have been known to get

We've done it! I'm happy and relieved after we finish an outstanding Grand Prix test.

lost and do several more before realizing they're in the midst of the Special, not the Grand Prix. And sometimes, even if you don't lose count, it's hard to get the horse to stop if he's on a roll.

After the "ones," which are clean, I make a turn down the centerline and prepare for the right pirouette. As I'm approaching my objective, I'm thinking I definitely want to make sure I have a little bend as I'm coming on centerline. I don't let the haunches come to the inside off the centerline before I start the pirouette. Two to three strides before I start the pirouette is when I really ask for that more collected pirouette canter. I need to feel Brentina sit down and be on the spot, waiting for the moment when I know she's really carrying herself.

At the letter L, I do a single pirouette. I tell myself not to get in a hurry, taking it a stride at a time. I don't think of it as one moment, but rather more as slices of a pie, focusing to make sure I don't over-rotate, looking at the judge's stand as I turn. A stride before the full pirouette is complete, I actually think about getting out of it, because you're on the straight line by the time the thought has gone through your mind.

So it's collected canter out, a flying change at X and then I think about the left pirouette coming up at I—making sure it has the same dimensions as the right pirouette. I'm focusing on not being in a hurry, keeping the balance; trying to look around the pirouette and seeking the straight line coming out. A stride before it's finished, again I think about exiting so I don't over-rotate. Then it's straight ahead in a collected canter, and track left.

At letter H, the first letter out of the corner, we immediately trot. By now, the horses know this so well, which means, as always, you have to be careful that there's no anticipation of the next movement.

The collected trot takes us to S, where we pick up the extended trot to F. This is where I have to be cautious with Brentina. She loves to go at this moment and I don't want her to get ahead of me and make a little stutter-step. Then it's a turn down the centerline and at the first letter, D, I half-halt with my legs at the girth to ask for passage.

At X, it's the piaffe transition. In this test, that is her best piaffe, because she's a little jacked-up. She knows this is getting close to the end, and that last extended trot can get a horse razzed.

Now it's time for our final passage. This is my last chance to impress the judges, so if I'm going to take any gambles, I do it now. I try to get the last little bit out of her, while telling her in a voice so soft no one can hear it, "We've only got a few more steps."

Heading toward G, I do a nice half-halt and sit deep, closing my lower leg, prepare for the halt and salute. It's over, and I'm so excited, because I know this was a good, clean test. The crowd breaks into a roar. I smile, give the thumbs-up, blow a kiss and wave, but first, I lean over and hug Brentina, as I always do. I thank my guardian angel, my Mom, for being there in spirit and helping me enjoy those special moments of riding in my own country and having it go well. I'm so overwhelmed by what we've just accomplished and the applause from the crowd that I feel like jumping out of my skin. It's such a high, such a rush, and I know Brentina shares it. There's not much that feels better than this. I wish everyone could enjoy this kind of moment!

CHAPTER 14

Questions and Answers

YOUR CONNECTION

■ **QUESTION: How will I know when I'm riding through? Is there any kind of a test I can do to tell?**

■ **ANSWER:** If you can move from a straight line in the trot or canter into a shoulder-in and take it into haunches-in and back to shoulder-in, and the horse stays in the same frame and rhythm, he's totally connected. Then you're riding through.

■ **QUESTION: How do I know that my horse is truly collected and relaxed through his back?**

■ **ANSWER:** When your horse is truly collected and relaxed in his back, you feel as if there are moments when you are not doing anything except sitting there. The horse feels as if he is willing to stay in that collected state on his own without the help of your hands or legs to maintain it.

■ **QUESTION: How can you know that you have a balanced position, and thus set your horse up to remain balanced, when you don't have help on the ground?**

■ **ANSWER:** Ask yourself whether you are centered and feeling equal contact in both reins. It would be very helpful if you have mirrors. I know that I could not do what I do on my own without them. Also, check to make sure your stirrup leathers are even. Take them off regularly, moving the left one to the right side and vice versa. Sometimes the left one will stretch because of mounting and dismounting. Even though the numbers on the holes might indicate they are even, that is not always the case. Manufacturers do make leathers that are reinforced with nylon to prevent stretching.

Sometimes a rider will want uneven stirrups because she has uneven legs. I hear this all the time, but I have found that there is usually less than a quarter-inch difference in the length of such a person's legs.

You don't have to compensate for that with different-length stirrups, even though some riders who think that their legs are different lengths get used to riding with a longer stirrup

Here are questions from real-life riders and my solutions to them. Chances are, you'll find answers to situations you and your horse are facing now, or will have to handle in the future. Consider this chapter a little bit of extra help!

on one side. If you have this problem, ride without stirrups for a couple of minutes before picking them back up. That way, both legs hang nice and long at the horse's sides, and when you pick up the irons again, they will feel more even. This is also good for learning to stay in the middle of your horse.

■ **QUESTION: When I ride shoulder-in, I feel as if my horse is on the aids, but then at a certain point in the arena, he frequently spooks to the inside. How can I keep the connection and prevent the spook?**

■ **ANSWER:** It sounds as if the horse is ignoring your inside leg. If he is spooking toward the inside of the arena, you are not making enough of an impression on him with your leg. I would try riding a circle before the spook if you can anticipate it. Make your point with your inside leg in the circle, and then try again. If this still fails, try going from shoulder-in to renvers (haunches-out) and see if this will help with control of the shoulders and sensitivity to the leg.

■ **QUESTION: I feel like my horse is fishtailing, just like my car when I drive it through a puddle patch on the highway. How can I regain control?**

■ **ANSWER:** To avoid a situation where the haunches won't stay behind the shoulders and your horse fails to remain straight and connected, make sure you're riding the shoulders completely straight with equal reins. Don't correct the haunches, just lengthen and shorten in all three gaits until the horse stays between your legs and your hands.

SUBMISSION

■ **QUESTION: How do I keep my horse's attention if, for example, someone comes out of the barn or an engine nearby starts up, and he gets so distracted he doesn't even know I'm on his back? What do you do if this happens at a show?**

■ **ANSWER:** The answer to this question starts at home. This is all about what we call submission. If you have a horse who acts this way, you need to make sure you have his full attention. When something happens that gets the horse started, you should address it by doing transitions. Bring the horse back, then leg-yield or circle, whichever will give you the most control for the moment. Whatever you do, don't run the horse forward; that only gives him the advantage in this situation.

Insist that the horse listens to the half-halt. It might be that he gets so fired up that you are afraid to bring him all the way to the walk for fear he will buck you off. If the horse is ready to uncork, keep moving. Try another leg-yield, or, if you and your horse are more advanced, haunches-out or haunches-in. You really have to experiment to see what gives you the best results. Once you have gotten his attention, continue with your work. Try to set this situation up again so you can perfect your solutions before going into the show ring. Even though you will not be able to use these techniques in the arena, if the horse learns to pay attention to you time after time, it will become second nature, and you will be able to control him in training.

■ **QUESTION: Is a snapping tail a sign of resistance? Is it significant to a judge? Is there any way to prevent it?**

■ **ANSWER:** It is a sign that your horse has a mind of his own. It can also be a sign of pain somewhere. I would have a vet rule this out before doing much more. Judges do frown on this and where it will show up in the score the most is the submission category. If your horse has done this from the beginning, then chances are it will happen again at some point. It usually happens when the horse has to work a little harder or something is difficult for him to do. Most horses do get better with time and experience. But as I said earlier, some horses are just opinionated!

■ **QUESTION: What should I do when I give an aid, like a little inside leg, and the horse ignores me or even pushes against my leg? I have tried with and without spurs. This doesn't happen all the time.**

■ **ANSWER:** If your horse listens one time and not the second time, you need to let him know that he must respond the same way every time. I would suggest using the whip as a secondary aid. If you time your whip at the exact moment as you use your leg, it gives the effect of a little surprise. Your horse will get the idea if you do this enough. Timing is everything, so work on your independent aids.

■ **QUESTION: My horse doesn't want me to put my leg on him. Even when I barely touch him, he overreacts and acts as if I walloped him.**

■ **ANSWER:** This falls in the same category as the horse who doesn't react. It is all about submission. Your horse, to some degree, must become de-sensitized. You can start at the walk and gently rub your horse's sides with the calves of your legs. When he gets accustomed to this, try applying the aids for the trot. If he steps off nicely, reward him, walk and start over again. Then in the walk, start to do shoulder-in and leg-yield. When he knows all of this, try haunches-in and half-pass at the walk. He just needs to get over the fact that you are going to use your leg. So don't baby him. Go ahead and use those legs! He will get over it in time.

TRAINING TIME

■ **QUESTION: How much time should I spend practicing each movement? When do you know the right time to quit or whether to keep working?**

■ **ANSWER:** The most important thing to remember is that you must keep it fair. Horses need to learn the movements, but they do not need to do them perfectly the first day when they are learning. Horses are not so different from people; you get better at something the more you do it, and so do they. But if you have ever learned a new sport, you also can appreciate that you get sore and cannot be an Olympic champion in one day.

You should never continue training a movement just for fun. Quality is your goal; Rome was not built in a day! When teaching a new movement, quit when you think he is getting the concept—even something as simple as moving away from your leg—rather than drilling and repeating it over and over until he gets frustrated, bored, sour or sore.

- **QUESTION:** What are some good exercises that should be included with every practice session?

- **ANSWER:** Concentrate on the suppleness to both sides and quality of the gaits. These are things I do every day with all of my horses. Basic work includes circles to both sides and serpentines in walk, trot and canter. The effectiveness of your transitions will tell you if your horse is on the aids. Once you have determined that the preliminaries are going well, move on to the leg-yield, shoulder-in and haunches-in. You can also do these in the walk, trot and canter.

SUPPLENESS

- **QUESTION:** How do you develop suppleness? What exercises are best for warming up?

- **ANSWER:** When I warm up my horses, I like to do serpentines and circles to make sure that they feel equal on both sides. Every horse will have a stiff side. You need to address it in the warm-up, working on equal feel to both sides. Do lots of leg-yields in walk and trot, especially on the stiff side. This way, the horse learns to let go of the tension on the stiff side, which will give you a better contact on the opposite side. It is more often the issue that the horse doesn't take contact on one side, rather than his being generally heavy or stiff. You need to work for an even connection, so when you start to do the movements, your horse is equal in the reins and regular in the gait without tension.

- **QUESTION:** My horse is stiff in the back. How do I get him to loosen up and go forward? This is not a soundness issue, as our vet has checked out the horse.

- **ANSWER:** I like to use the rising trot when the horse is tight and not moving forward. Sometimes when you try to sit prematurely during the trot, the horse just gets tighter. I will go back to basic transitions (walk, trot, canter) until I feel that the horse is swinging in his back again. Whatever you do, try not to force the issue by pushing the horse more forward. This will only make the situation worse.

MOUTH TROUBLE

- **QUESTION:** When your horse plays with the bit and fusses, and you lose contact as a result, what should you do?

- **ANSWER:** Make sure your horse does not have a dental problem. Then check to see if the bit is too low in his mouth. That would make it uncomfortable for the horse to hold the bit properly. Most people try to throw the contact away when the horse fusses, but you really need to take more feel. However, you have to know how much feel you can take without upsetting your horse. Do a lot of transitions if your horse is playing with the bit. Walk-trot and trot-walk transitions seem to work best. Leg-yields also will help the horse get a better connection on the outside rein. Do not get into a pulling match!

■ **QUESTION: My horse seems to foam more on one side of his mouth than the other—is there something wrong?**

■ **ANSWER:** Not necessarily, but I would make sure that your vet checks the horse's teeth on a regular six-month schedule. A rider's uneven hands can also cause this.

USING THE HIND END

■ **QUESTION: My horse is very long in the back. Often, I have trouble getting him to use his hind end and get it under him. Any thoughts?**

■ **ANSWER:** If this is a conformational thing, then you might always have a problem with this. Remember that not every horse can be a Grand Prix horse. You must be honest with yourself and kind to the horse. But what will help with this problem are lots of transitions to get the horse stronger and more active in his hind end.

The secret here is trying to limit the transitional steps to as few as possible. Example: From trot to walk, do only a couple of steps walking and then go back to the trot. Do the same from trot to canter and back, with as few trot steps as possible and then the same with canter-walk. It will help the horse become quicker and stronger in his hind end. This will also help increase the horse's sensitivity to the aids.

DROPPING THE SHOULDER

■ **QUESTION: My horse drops his shoulder out on one side. How can I correct this?**

■ **ANSWER:** Start by using a little counter-flexion to the side where the shoulder is falling out. When using counter-flexion, remember not to overbend the horse to the outside. You only want to establish more control of the outside shoulder. If your horse is more advanced, then you can also use a little haunches-out (renvers) in the trot to get better control of the outside shoulder. Be careful not to bend the neck too much to the inside, however, as it will cause the shoulder to fall out even more.

ABOVE THE BIT

■ **QUESTION: My horse often goes above the bit, and I get very frustrated trying to fix it. Frankly, most of the time I can't, and he wins.**

■ **ANSWER:** When a horse goes above the bit to avoid contact, take a feel, ride on a 10-meter clockwise circle in the walk, leg-yielding to the outside and trying to get the horse connected on the outside rein. Think "a little sideways" until the horse gives it up and becomes rounder. If he starts to run through the outside of the circle, simply change direction and go counter-clockwise, tapping him lightly with the whip if necessary to encourage the hind legs to step to the contact. When the horse starts to accept the connection, and become rounder, let him walk straight for a few steps. Then repeat the exercise until he comes forward into the hand and stretches down, almost as if he wanted to go long and low. When the exercise is completed at the walk, try it at the trot. Remember to have patience. It could take some time to change the pattern that has become familiar to him.

A BETTER TOPLINE

■ **QUESTION: What's the best way to develop my horse's topline?**

■ **ANSWER:** This should be done through proper stretching and connection. Start by doing several upward and downward transitions to get a better connection. As the horse accepts the contact, he will soften the topline, stretch and therefore be able to develop the muscles. The topline is the muscle structure on the top of the horse's neck and back. Why is it so important? These are the muscles that the horse needs to do the higher levels of dressage. These muscles will help protect the horse from injuries and strain on tendons and ligaments. How long does it take to develop a good topline? It takes several years for a Grand Prix horse.

THE WALK

■ **QUESTION: My horse jigs at the walk in his dressage test because he gets hyped up. How do I achieve a calm walk in the arena? He's okay with it when I do the test at home. Sometimes he steps into the tracks of his front feet. Other times, he doesn't. How can I make him step more under himself at the walk?**

■ **ANSWER:** I know exactly what you mean. I don't think that any dressage rider hasn't had this problem at one time or another. First of all, you want to make sure that you can get your horse to listen to the half-halt enough that you don't have to hold him too strongly in the hand. But if this only happens at the show, and your horse has a good walk at home, he needs to go on the road more often. This doesn't mean you need to show the legs off the horse. It just means he needs to be away from home more. When your horse is not so star-struck, the good walk you have at home should show up in the arena.

The walk is the easiest gait to destroy. If you have real problems with getting the horse to step under himself, you'll need a professional's eye to help you. In the meantime, try taking the horse on the trails and getting the best relaxed walk from him that you can. That way, both you and he will know what it feels like. However, if the horse doesn't naturally have a big overstep, exercises won't help. Watch him when he's loose in the paddock. If he doesn't have a natural overstep there, you'll never be able to change that, no matter what you do. Try to concentrate instead on other aspects of your performance together.

THE CANTER

■ **QUESTION: My horse was taught to canter from a spur aid, not a leg. How do I correct this?**

■ **ANSWER:** If the horse does not respond to a light leg, use a firm bump of the leg and a light tap with the whip in the moment of the transition. It will take many repetitions for your horse to realize this is the proper aid. Be patient, but be careful to use the flat part of your lower leg and not turn your toes out when applying your aids. You are trying to teach your horse to listen to a whisper, not a shout.

■ **QUESTION: I can get my horse to canter from the walk but he won't canter from the trot in one direction. What should I do?**

ANSWER: More than likely, he is behind your leg. Try to do some forward and back transitions within the trot before attempting the canter. This will encourage the horse to think more forward in the transition and therefore make it possible to have a good canter depart from the walk. Also make sure that you are not bending the horse too much in the neck and that you are careful where your leg is positioned for the transition. Remember to move your inside leg slightly forward as you move your outside leg slightly back. Pay attention to your seat, so you don't lean forward or to the inside.

QUESTION: In the flying change, my horse very often changes late behind. Is there anything I can do to make her more prompt?

ANSWER: You have to remember that "late behind" means the horse is not sensitive to the leg. "Late in front" usually means the horse is blocked in the shoulders because of the rider's hands. I would suggest doing more transitions to get the horse more sensitive to your leg. That way, when you move your leg back for the change, the horse is sharp off the aids. Doing simple transitions to walk is best in this situation. Slowly keep limiting the number of walk steps before the canter.

QUESTION: How do you get your horse to remain straight and balanced through the canter, while avoiding having him swing his haunches in?

ANSWER: If your horse is swinging his haunches, then you know that he is not truly connected from back to front. Do not try fixing the haunches; the shoulders are the problem. You might be holding too much bend and forcing him to compensate and balance himself by moving his haunches in. Do more transitions from trot to canter and make sure to stay off the rail. That way, you don't have the rail to act as, in effect, an outside rein. You must make sure that the horse is truly straight between your own hands and legs.

When you depart to the canter, see if the horse tends to throw his shoulders toward the rail. If he does, that is your problem. You need to make sure your departure is straight to keep the horse truly straight in the canter. To fix this, start from trot to canter. If you notice that the horse is moving his shoulders to the outside and his haunches to the inside at the trot, try some transitions from walk to trot. It is important that the horse is thinking forward in this exercise. You can also do some renvers at trot, straighten and then try again. It's like driving a car on the ice—if you keep the brake on, the car goes more sideways. Use forward and back to get the horse straight before trying the canter again.

QUESTION: I'm having trouble picking up the canter from the walk. Very often, my horse trots a few steps (or more) before he goes into the canter.

ANSWER: The walk-to-canter transition is very important. When asked to go into the canter from the collected walk, a lot of riders immediately start to fidget, perhaps taking up their reins a little more, adjusting their position or pulling the horse's head to the inside, thinking they have to do something when they're actually already set up perfectly for a canter transition.

You should be able to go from a collected walk, keeping the horse straight, and pick up the canter. When a rider over-prepares, the horse will become tense, jig or become crooked. This is a good example of the saying, "less is more." Teach your horse to listen to a whisper of your leg. When riders have to use too much leg for a canter transition, they wind up having to deal with correcting crookedness. You don't have to make a big move to go from the collected walk to the canter.

Mistakes that come up in the transition include letting the horse go when you put your leg on, which produces a trot step because you're not keeping enough feel in your hand. I also see a tendency in some riders to tip forward and let the hand go, losing the connection. Practice halting, walking two steps and then cantering just a few strides before coming back gracefully to the walk.

MORE TRANSITION TROUBLE

■ **QUESTION: My horse seems to lose his balance in the downward transitions. What can I do to help him?**

■ **ANSWER:** You must make sure that you are not holding him too much with the reins before the transition. Lots of forward and back within the gait will help you achieve this balance better. Set your horse up for the transition and then leave him alone and try not to disturb the balance by riding too strongly.

LEG-YIELD

■ **QUESTION: I'm having trouble achieving a good leg-yield with my horse.**

■ **ANSWER:** A good exercise for preparing a leg-yield involves the walk circle. Use the circle to create a bend, then ask your horse to step away from your inside leg on the circle. Until the horse starts to move away from the leg, continue a little bit of pressure, also using your secondary aid, the whip. The minute he responds at all to what you want, take the pressure off and get back on the original circle. Then try it again and ask a little more, moving sideways for a longer period.

SHOULDER-IN

■ **QUESTION: My horse won't hold the shoulder-in the entire length of the arena. What should I do?**

■ **ANSWER:** Chances are that he really is not listening to your half-halts. Go back to basics again, paying close attention to the half-halts. You're better off breaking up your shoulder-in work, anyway, rather than doing it the entire length of the arena. Going down the long side, take the horse from a shoulder-in position into a 10-meter circle halfway down the rail, at E or B, then go back into the shoulder-in. That way, your horse doesn't have to do the exercise for such a long stretch, which should help you maintain the quality.

THE HALF-PASS

- **QUESTION: In a half-pass, my horse tends to make too steep an angle and I sometimes wind up with the haunches leading. What am I doing wrong?**

- **ANSWER:** You are not in control of the shoulders. Can you do haunches-in on the long side? Then you can do haunches-in on the diagonal. That is what a half-pass is! Whatever line you choose to ride, think of it as nothing more than haunches-in on that line. Work on controlling the shoulders on that diagonal line, and use your inside leg to encourage the horse to step forward.

- **QUESTION: I'm just not getting the half-pass. Is there anything I can do to make my attempts easier on my horse and me?**

- **ANSWER:** Too often, you say "half-pass" to a rider and she comes out of the corner pushing and shoving the horse from the outside leg, trying to get him to go sideways. That makes the horse tight in the back. Simplify half-pass for your horse by teaching him haunches-in on a diagonal line. That way, the shoulder is always leading, which gives the horse a place to go and means he is always thinking "forward." If you start pushing the horse sideways, he may lose quality in the trot. In the haunches-in on the diagonal, it is easy to keep the quality supple and lovely. By using the longer diagonal line, you are forced to use your inside leg to keep it from becoming too steep. When you lose the quality get out of the movement, regain it and then try again.

    Start with shoulder-in, straighten, then go into the haunches-in. This can be done in either the trot or canter. The goal is to be able to go from one to the other without losing the quality of the gait, which you can regain when you straighten. This helps improve the degree of collection and suppleness. The horse should be able to stay on the same track. The exercise shows control of the shoulders. (See diagram page 48.)

    A lot of horses have a spectacular trot, but when they go into a half-pass, they move like ponies because they can't hold the cadence and rhythm when doing lateral movements. That problem is all connection-related—a sign the horse isn't truly connected from back to front. When the horse is truly connected and on the aids, that doesn't happen.

PASSAGE

- **QUESTION: How do you know that you are working the passage correctly when you are training on your own and don't have ground help?**

- **ANSWER:** When working on passage, I think about the reaction to my aids. If you need to be holding too strongly with your hands or legs, then the horse is not truly doing a passage. You need to work on the transition more than the length of time in the movement. Remember to bring the horse back with a half-halt and your legs at the girth to keep the activity. When the horse is sensitive to the aids (both forward and back) then it should not require more than this to make it happen. When you bring the horse back and he gets heavier in the hand, a slight tap with the whip behind should be more than sufficient to generate some suspension. When you feel as if the horse is doing it for himself without your support, then chances are it is good. Remember that a horse becomes irregular from the rider holding him too strongly with her hands or using her legs too much to keep him in passage. Don't do passage for a long period of time when you're training. It is important that the horse not feel it is a punishment, but just part of his normal, everyday work. That is why I start my horses when they are young to just come back in the trot and learn to give me a moment of suspension. That way, it is only a matter of time and increasing strength until it develops into a true passage.

PIROUETTE

■ **QUESTION: In the walk pirouette, I get halfway through it and my horse stalls and it becomes a turn on the forehand. Why does this happen?**

■ **ANSWER:** Your horse is not really in front of your leg. You need to prepare *as if* you were going to do the pirouette, and then walk on. Pay close attention to your horse's tempo. When you feel him shutting down, bump him with your leg and even give him a tap with the whip. But whatever you do, do not continue with the turning phase of the pirouette, which will just give your horse a chance to get away from you. Teach him to keep the rhythm and not fall behind your leg. Start with just a couple of steps, making sure you can get out of it and he walks on when you ask him to. You want to train your horse with a light leg, even taking it away sometimes to make sure that he is going on his own. If he should shut down, this is the time when you need to let him know that he must walk on!

Brentina demonstrates a nice bend in the half-pass here as we school at home in Idaho.

CHAPTER 15

I Reach My Goal

So HERE IT WAS FINALLY, 2004, THE YEAR WE hoped we would reach our goal: The Olympics. This ultimate sporting event was to be held during the summer in Athens, ancient home of the Olympics. Could it be any more exciting than this?

But there was a lot to do in the months before the Games, starting with the World Cup finals. Because I had been elevated to the World Cup title in 2003 after winner Ulla Salzgeber's horse, Rusty, was disqualified for a positive drug test, I automatically was qualified for the finals.

While I didn't have to do our national freestyle championship, the U.S. League World Cup qualifier, we decided to participate anyway. It was in Burbank, California, close to our winter base, and Brentina had enjoyed a long rest. It was time to get her involved in competition again.

Riding in the Athens Olympics was the culmination of a dream.

She won the freestyle championship and we planned to do one more show before the World Cup after we flew to Europe. The show was in Dortmund, Germany. The location was a brand-new building with the most pathetic footing you've ever seen. It was two-foot-deep motocross dirt and clay, with sand scattered on top of it. Every single rider said, "I'm leaving."

So the organizers canceled the first day of the show and took out half of the clay, covering it with rock sand and putting regular sand on top of that. I had a gut feeling it still was not right, and I should have stuck with that. But there is pressure at a competition like this, and the other riders were going to participate. I thought maybe I was just being overly cautious, especially since the arena people did everything possible to make it right for me. They scheduled me to ride just after the break, when they'd rolled it again. I went ahead, and won the Grand Prix. The Special was in the old arena, where there was great footing, so we did that and won it, too.

But the next morning, Brentina's right hind leg was swollen. Although everyone was trying to make light of it, I knew something was going on there that wasn't good.

We had the fabulous German veterinarian, Dr. Peter Cronau, come out to Klaus's place to ultrasound the leg. After he finished, I felt a knot in my stomach that wasn't relieved by what he told us: "The good news is, I think you'll be fine for the Olympics. The bad news is, you're not going to the World Cup—I found some torn fibers in the superficial flexor tendon." There we were, stuck in Germany, just wanting to go home.

But if we had gone home, we would have looked like poor sports. I gritted my teeth and went to the World Cup finals in Dusseldorf to support Leslie Morse and Guenter Seidel, our other riders at the Cup. I tried to keep my chin up, but it was really hard. As the competition went on around me, I was counting the minutes until it was over and we could go back to the U.S.

At our winter base in California, we had Brentina's leg ultrasounded once more to check the progress of the healing, and the first prognosis was not very optimistic at all. In fact, the veterinarian there thought he saw a change for the worse, and doubted the Olympics were going to happen for us—after we had waited so long and worked so hard for a chance to go.

That was when Bob flew in our local vet, Dr. George Martin, from Idaho, and consulted ultrasound expert Dr. Norman Rantanen. He did a thorough diagnostic work-up on Brentina. Clinically, Dr. Rantanen told us, there were no symptoms whatsoever. In other words, she was not lame, but there *were* changes in the ultrasound. The vet comforted us by saying there were horses running races out there with far worse ultrasounds.

Dr. Rantanen was quite optimistic that with a good plan, we could reach our goal. Since Brentina was a mare who knew her job, all we had to do was keep her exercised. We realized we'd have to cope with a little lack of fitness because we couldn't work her the way we normally would before a big competition.

Luckily, the mare was given a bye by the U.S. federation, meaning she didn't have to compete in the selection trials, in the hopes that she would be fine with a bit more rest.

We would go to Europe with the plan that she was to take part in a single show prior to the Olympics, just to prove she was fit enough to get through the competition.

But what a show we had to compete in—Aachen, one of the world's most celebrated venues. I rode very conservatively there, being careful to do nothing extravagant, and we finished fourth. It was only one week after I had done my first canter pirouette in nearly four months, and there were just a few weeks left until the Olympics, which would be the biggest test ever of Brentina's prowess and my riding ability.

It certainly wasn't the ideal scenario for success. Everybody had all the faith in the world in the horse and they seemed to have faith in me, too, though I didn't have a whole lot of faith in myself.

Frankly, I didn't know if I could handle that kind of pressure, especially with all the hype about the mare and my chance for an individual medal. My biggest fear was that I would be a hindrance to the team; I wasn't even thinking of an individual medal at this point.

But all the riders and team officials were willing to take a gamble on the mare because of her past history of reliability. In Greece, we tuned up as much as we could, walking a fine line between doing too little and doing too much. Roger Wilkinson, our shoer from Idaho, came over with a special bar shoe he had made that gave her tendon more support. It hung out behind her hoof, and wasn't pretty. Right before we competed, though, he cut it back so it wasn't quite as obvious.

On Grand Prix day at the equestrian venue, with all the flags flying and flapping in the breeze, Brentina once again showed her heart by going in there and giving it everything she had. The heat was extreme, the pressure was intense, and still, she never said no.

Our score of 73.375 percent was the highest for the U.S. team. The mare had led the way to a bronze medal. Once I knew my score was one that would help the team, and not hinder it, that was a relief for me.

Actually, I was ecstatic about the ride until I watched a couple of the other tests later that I thought were scored too high.

I was riding a horse who had been injured and done very little preparation compared to the other horses, but nonetheless she put in a very accurate test. How could horses that jumped out of their skin and practically left the arena still be given higher marks?

At that moment, I wanted to pack up and go home, but in those circumstances, that's not a possibility. What do you do when you feel like I felt in Greece? I realized it was the same scenario as in the past; business as usual. I just had to do the job that I was sent to do and not let things get to me.

When you're a role model for those coming up in dressage, it's your job to be a good sport, whether or not you got the score you thought you deserved. You put a smile on your face and try to keep going. You don't have the luxury of acting like a spoiled brat and having a temper tantrum. Believe me, a lot of things are going on in your mind at a time like that—things you'd love to do and say, but you can't. You simply have to bite your tongue and go on.

After the Grand Prix, I was standing fifth individually, and there was a bit of a break before the Special, the next step on the road to the individual medals.

What was really difficult was to stay "up." I

I celebrated my 50th birthday at a party during the Athens Olympics.

The 2004 Olympic bronze medal team: Robert Dover, Lisa Wilcox, me! and Guenter Seidel tried very hard to keep away from the press in Greece. Everyone was asking me, "Now, what do you think your chances are for an individual medal?"

That was something I didn't want to talk about, let alone listen to. All I wanted to say was, "I'm just thankful I'm here. This shows what type of horse Brentina is. She's unbeatable as far as her qualities and what you can expect from her."

But the judges don't take that kind of thing into account.

In the Special, the mare put in a consistent test to finish fourth with 74.760 percent. By then, the other horses that hadn't had the best performances in the Grand Prix (but got scored high anyway) actually did better tests in the Special. In my opinion, though, some of them shouldn't have even qualified for the Special, while some riders from other countries had good rides that didn't seem to be rewarded.

I really felt for them, as well as for myself, because everyone works so hard to get to that point. Making it to the Olympics is such a special thing. All any of us would like is fair judging, and I'm not sure we always get that.

My overall total after the Special was 74.067 percent, making me fourth in the standings. Going into the freestyle, it looked as if there was a slim chance we could possibly get a medal but I knew after what had occurred the two previous days that was not going to happen.

I'm usually so excited to do the freestyle, which Brentina and I perform so well, but when I woke up that morning, everything felt flat.

> *Going into the freestyle, it looked as if there was a slim chance we could possibly get a medal, but I knew after what had occurred the two previous days that was not going to happen.*

The experience of being at the Olympics was everything I hoped it would be. I made up my mind to enjoy being part of the opening ceremonies in Athens and for one evening, put aside my thoughts about the competition in which I would take part a few days later.

In preparation for the opening ceremony the athletes sat in a holding stadium where we were seated by country.

There was a giant TV screen that showed what was happening in the main stadium, but it was hard to see what was going on. After hours of waiting, the drama unfolded really fast. All the teams were led through a maze of trails into a tunnel. There was a feeling like thunder rumbling in my body as my heart beat faster and faster the closer I got to the main stadium. When the U.S. team arrived in the stadium to a roar of welcome, that was a relief. None of us knew how we would be received with the international situation the way it was. What a feeling it was to march into that stadium with I don't know how many people waving flags!

My goal was to get to the inside or the outside of lines of marchers so my friends at home could see me on TV. But I was surrounded by so many tall people that no one could have ever seen me!

This night of opening ceremonies was magic. It was wonderful to see how the world can be at peace, even if only for the Olympics. As we stood in the center of the stadium, we talked with athletes of so many different countries, some of which I had never even heard of. I was in awe of the number of different languages and colorful native costumes.

As we mixed, mingled and took pictures, I looked around and saw that officials were trying to keep a spot clear in the center of the stadium. I said to my teammates, "Guys, we need to get over there; that's where something is going to happen." So we headed in that direction and sure enough, up came this platform where the officials were going to speak, and we had a great view for the whole show, something I will never forget.

Just after we awakened, I told Bob, "I've worked so hard to get to the Olympics. This is the moment I should be most excited for, and I can't get up for this ride. I don't even want to go down that centerline."

How easily I could have not shown up that day, gotten on a plane, gone home and not thought twice about it. I felt like I'd just been beaten up. It was an emotion I hadn't encountered before, even at the WEG in Spain.

To some extent, although the judging was out of my control, I felt as if I had let so many people down. I knew what the USET and USEF were hoping for, what the press was hoping for, what my hometown fans who got up at 3 a.m. to watch the freestyle on TV were hoping for, and I realized I wouldn't be able to deliver.

Although I wondered then whether it would have made a difference if the mare hadn't gotten injured earlier that year, I honestly think that wouldn't have changed anything.

The freestyle at the Olympics was far from my best effort. It felt like an out-of-body experience, as I had some very uncharacteristic errors in the one-tempis—I just couldn't get myself in the tunnel of focus. I had to stop them because I couldn't keep up with the rhythm, then start them again.

To this day, I haven't ever watched the video of that freestyle, and I didn't read the comments on my test.

I knew what I did. The judges had a place they wanted to put me, and I gave them an opening. We were marked at 78.825 percent for the freestyle, bringing my total for the Olympics to 75.653, only a little more than 1 percent from a medal. Fourth again.

That night, there was a 50th birthday cake for me during a party at the house where a lot of team supporters stayed. After I blew out the candles, someone asked what I wished for.

"Health and happiness," I told her.

"Not a gold medal?" she asked.

"It's a little late for that," I replied.

But when you look at the big picture, being fourth in the Olympics wasn't so bad. Three months earlier, I hadn't even thought I would make the Games. After all we were part of a team effort that brought home a bronze medal.

I was so excited to finish third in the 2005 World Cup finals.

With the Olympics behind me, it was time for a break from competition, and I took a pretty long one. But then I had to get into gear again, because 2005 was an important year, too. For the first time, the show jumping and dressage World Cup finals would be held together, on the same weekend. And the venue was Las Vegas' Thomas & Mack Center, named for Parry Thomas and his late business partner, Jerry Mack.

Here I am celebrating Brentina's being named the 2006 Farnam/Platform U.S. Equestrian Federation Horse of the Year with USEF President David O'Connor, Jane Thomas and Farnam President Chris Jacobi.

For the World Cup Finals, I wanted to do something special, to send a message to the judges. So we came up with a new freestyle, built around the old Aretha Franklin tune, "Respect." That was what I needed and by gosh, I was going to get it.

Everyone loved it when I tried it out at the national freestyle championship. I was heading for Vegas, and I thought having the finals in our country might give me a chance to step up the ladder a little bit further, provided my ride was cleaner than someone else's.

I was rejuvenated by the World Cup, because I went in with a different attitude. I was riding for me, and for Brentina, just trying to do the best we could do, and bring that wonderful capacity audience of nearly 12,000 people along with us.

I thought the crowd was awesome, and I laughed and had fun. Dressage is supposed to be a "shhhh" sport, but I wanted them to join in with me. I shook my head, asking the eager fans to clap in rhythm as I went up the centerline, and they were happy to comply.

The mare liked it, though I thought she was a bit startled at this departure from the norm. She tried to stay with me, and said, "Okay Mom, I'll do it if you ask me, but they're awfully loud."

Things went well at the World Cup. I had no problem at all with finishing third behind Anky van Grunsven and Edward Gal, two riders from the Netherlands who had fabulous tests. It was great to be in that company, great to be considered in the top three with the others.

Actually, I was ecstatic. That's the ride I'll always have in my head, to replay and enjoy whenever I want to. The judges treated us fairly, which is all I ever asked for, and I hope it continues to stay on that path for the rest of the mare's career. I know how hard she tries, and when I feel she is treated unfairly, I take it personally, like a mother protecting her child. Brentina has definitely become a family member because of who and what she is—a very, very special horse who is a part of me, as much as I am a part of her.

CHAPTER 16

Another Medal:
The 2006 World Equestrian Games

As YOU KNOW FROM READING ABOUT MY LIFE with Brentina, her competitive career has been a bit of a roller coaster in recent years while we strive to keep her fit and sound. That's always more difficult with an older horse, but after the 2004 Olympics and the 2005 World Cup, we were hoping for smoother sailing.

Our next goal was the 2006 World Equestrian Games in Aachen, Germany, a location where we had shown several times previously. Aside from championships, Aachen is really "it" in the dressage world, the most important competition of the year to win.

We were saving Brentina for the big occasions, so she had a good rest after the World Cup finals, and then I was planning to prepare her for the WEG and the competitions required to qualify for it.

But in the fall of 2005, an ultrasound showed that Brentina was developing a tendon problem in a different place on the same leg that had bothered her before the Olympic.

Receiving our bronze medal with teammates Guenter Seidel, Steffen Peters and Leslie Morse

We put her into therapy immediately, of course, and she got plenty of rest. By the time we went to our California winter base in February 2006, I was riding her and she seemed perfectly fine, though her program was still an easy one. We knew that it wouldn't take much to get her qualified for the WEG, and I was determined to ask for a bye from the June selection trials at the USEF national championships in Gladstone, New Jersey. Although I love the beautiful home of the U.S. Equestrian Team Foundation, Brentina has not adjusted well there—remember the time she got hives?

We finally determined that the moment was right to compete, so in May, Brentina went to the Flintridge, California, show. Everything was done to accommodate her, and adjustments were made to the footing so she could be at her best without taking a risk.

Brentina won the Grand Prix there easily. She felt just fine, the way she always had, and

Talking to coach Klaus Balkenhol and USEF dressage manager Gil Merrick.

without pushing her I could sense that she was ready to be a star again. We didn't do the Grand Prix Special at Flintridge. It just wasn't necessary, since the one class had qualified us for the WEG.

I went to Gladstone myself, however, to support the other riders and award the first Brentina Cup to Elisabeth Austin (see page 74). This competition, originally called the Passage Cup, was designed to bridge the gap between Young Riders and the professional ranks for the up-and-coming people in our sport. Peggy and Parry Thomas liked the idea so much they decided to fund it, and re-name it after Brentina.

I had never gotten an official okay that Brentina would be part of the team without going in the trials, but I knew Klaus wanted her on the squad. Steffen Peters and Guenter Seidel had made the team by finishing first and second at the trials with Floriano and Aragon, so they were all set. Finally, I was told that I would be going with them to Germany, where we would train at Klaus's place and compete in several shows. Several other riders also were named to the short list, so we had quite a big group of Americans spending time together in Germany.

In preparation for the WEG, before the team was named, I competed at a German national show, Elmlohe. Brentina won the Grand Prix with a score of more than 76 percent and Klaus was beaming. Because of her excellent result, he said she did not have to compete at Verden, an international show in Germany, as originally scheduled for a pre-WEG prep.

We were set. Brentina got named to the team and my troubles were behind me, I thought. All we had to do was keep her in work and focus on getting a medal at the WEG. Because Olympic champion Anky van Grunsven of the Netherlands was receiving astronomical scores with Keltec Salinero, we knew the Dutch team would be buoyed by her marks. It therefore seemed unlikely that we would get another silver medal, as we had in Jerez when the Dutch team was much weaker. As usual, it was taken for granted that Germany would be getting the gold.

But we had big competition from the Danes for the bronze. They had a secret weapon—Blue Hors Matine, a fabulous gray mare ridden by the gifted Andreas Helgstrand. Few people knew how good this horse is. Andreas was supposed to bring a more experienced mount to the WEG, but when that horse went lame, he decided to take a chance with Matine. We needed to get the bronze to

Marching along with the other U.S. athletes during the opening ceremonies.

qualify for the 2008 Olympics. If we weren't in the top three at the WEG, our next, and only, chance would be the 2007 Pan American Games. They were being held at Intermediaire I level, so it would have put a lot of pressure on whoever made the team there if they had to worry about Olympic qualification.

Finally, we arrived at Aachen, where the showgrounds were even more impressive than they are for the annual international competition there. I had a great time marching in the fabulous opening ceremonies, which were done so lavishly it seemed as if we were at the Olympics. There were more than 40,000 fans in the stands cheering, and I felt revved up, ready to do my best to get a medal for the USA.

Brentina was to go last for our team in the Grand Prix, because that's the way Klaus wanted it, and I wasn't in a position to say no—even though I hate being the anchor rider.

On the first day of competition, I was on hand to cheer for Guenter, who performed capably to give us a nice start with a score of 69.792.

On the second day, it was our turn to step up to the plate. Steffen rode in the morning, and we all breathed a sigh of relief when he had a beautiful test with Floriano, who seemed to get better and better every time he competed. He wound up with 72.708 percentage points, which would be good enough for sixth place individually.

I was confident as I warmed up, noting how wonderful Brentina felt. But shortly after I entered the arena, saluted the judges and started my test, I thought I felt something that was not quite right in the first extended trot. But I knew I had a job to do in there, so I tried to stay focused on that. I rode conservatively, to make sure Brentina didn't hurt herself, but in the last extended trot I could definitely feel she wasn't 100 percent. Though my heart was in my throat, there was no time to panic. Once again, I found myself riding through adversity. And Brentina, being the lady she is, came down that centerline toward the final halt with great vigor and energy, giving me everything she had while showing the judges that she still shone with star quality.

We wound up with a score of 71.417 percentage points, putting us ninth individually, but most important, the team won the bronze with 213.917 percentage points. That put us a comfortable distance in front of the Danes, who had 208.874 percentage points.

It was quite something to climb up on the podium in front of all those knowledgeable spectators in Aachen and accept the team bronze medal.

I breathed a big sigh of relief after we finished our test in the Grand Prix and I could give Brentina a pat.

Everyone was watching us at the trot-up as I jogged Brentina for the judges.

We trained in the empty stadium so our horses could get used to the venue.

"Mission accomplished," I thought, knowing that we had qualified for the Olympics. It was a tumultuous afternoon. I felt a mixture of pride, relief and worry, hoping Brentina was okay and that we weren't going to be dealing with anything serious.

Of course, we had the veterinarians go over her right away, but nothing showed up immediately. The next day, however, there was a little filling in the leg. At that point, we decided it would be in her best interests to call it a day at the WEG, since she has nothing to prove to anybody. So I scratched from the Grand Prix Special, and that was the end of our WEG, since we'd done what we came for.

Everyone was asking me if she would ever compete again. I couldn't really answer that question without a complete veterinary work-up, which was something we could only get at home.

Looking back on the WEG, I have mixed emotions. I was disappointed not to be able to ride in the individual competitions, but I am so proud to have been a part of the team bronze medal and also about the fact that we secured a spot for the next Olympics.

At times like these, you have to focus on the big picture. I feel so lucky in my life to have been able to do the things I love and meet amazing people along the way. I hope you have enjoyed the journey with us!

Here I am in the VIP section of the stands with Parry and Peggy Thomas.

As always, Brentina gave me everything she had during our test, but I played it conservative—we weren't taking any chances on losing the bronze medal.

S O THERE YOU ARE. THAT'S AN OVERVIEW OF DRESSAGE, AS I SEE IT. I HOPE THIS all has been helpful, but don't forget, you need a good trainer, or at the very least, a good eye on the ground, if you're going to advance very far in this discipline. But now you should have a better idea of the training basics and what it takes to progress with your horse.

This has been fun (and truthfully, a lot of work!), telling you what I've learned over a relatively short period, as dressage careers go. May your experiences all be fruitful and fulfilling, for your horse as well as for you.

As for me, I'm not sure what the future will bring. Brentina and I should be around in the arena a while longer, maybe even doing a few exhibitions after she retires from the show ring. After that, she'll always have green pastures to enjoy. Whatever I'm doing at that point, I know it will involve being with horses and helping others to learn what "riding through" is all about.

All my best wishes for your success and enjoyment,

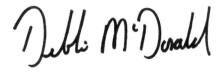

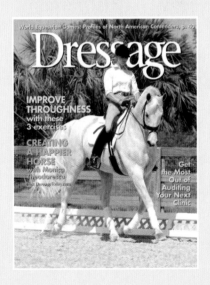